Collector's Guide to
Raphael Tuck & Sons

Paper Dolls, Paper Toys & Children's Books

by
Blair & Margaret Whitton

Published by Hobby House Press Cumberland, MD 21502

Additional copies of this book may be purchased at $24.95
from
Hobby House Press
900 Frederick Street
Cumberland, Maryland 21502
or from your favorite bookstore or dealer.
Please add $5.50 per copy for postage.

Printed in the United States of America
ISBN: 0-87588-370-2

Table of Contents

Dedication

To Barbara Whitton Berger, our daughter, who encouraged us to continue her research into the Raphael Tuck & Sons, Ltd.

Acknowledgements

Very few research books are successful without the cooperation and support of many people and institutions who are willing to share their collections and their knowledge with us. This book is no exception. Our heartfelt thanks to Maurine Popp, Peggy Jo Rosamond, Jan Banneck, Herbert Hosmer, Joyce Alexander, Jean Woodcock, Grace Piemontesi, Marlene Brenner, Marlys Clark, Richard Merrill, Judith Lassalle, Anne Williams, Vicky Pagan, Lynn Murray, Marion Jennings, Barbara and Joseph Berger and William Nutting.

We would also like to thank Christine Mosser of the Metropolitan Toronto Reference Library, Larry E. Weiler of the Ontario Ministry of Culture and Communications, and Clarke Christy of the Manuscript Division of the National Archives of Canada. They all helped us tremendously in researching the Raphael Tuck & Sons Co., in Canada.

Unless otherwise noted, all paper dolls, books and paper toys are from the collection of Blair and Margaret Whitton.

This book contains more than 300 photographs of paper collectibles. In some instances, several photographs are used to fully-illustrate an item.

Introduction

Researching the Raphael Tuck & Sons Company has been both frustrating and rewarding. To come up with what we might refer to as a complete history of this company is an impossible task.

In 1969, our daughter Barbara Berger (Jendrick) contacted the Tuck company in preparation for her book about this very prolific company. At this point we would like to quote from her introduction in her book titled *Paper Dolls and Paper Toys of Raphael Tuck & Sons.*

"Those of us who are interested in Raphael Tuck paper dolls and toys know that there is an almost total lack of information on the subject. This is due in part to the fact that the company headquarters of Tuck was in London and it was completely bombed out during World War II.

"In August of 1960 I wrote to the Raphael Tuck Company in London asking for any information that they might have. They did not seem to know anything about the paper dolls. They sent me a history of the Tuck firm titled "The Romance of Raphael Tuck & Sons Ltd. Published on the Occasion of the Company's Centenary."

We have incorporated some of the information from this history plus placing a strong influence on the juvenile side of the works published by Raphael Tuck & Sons. By this we mean that emphasis has been placed on paper toys, paper dolls and children's story books.

In the year 1866, Raphael and Ernestine Tuck opened a small shop selling prints and frames. Through hard work, dedication and long tedious hours, this small business developed into a thriving enterprise and by the end of the 19th century was known worldwide as a great publishing company.

This growing publishing giant was based in London and had branches in Paris, Berlin and New York before 1900 and later in Montreal and Toronto. As mentioned before, the subject matter of this study covers the growth of the firm, the paper toys and dolls they published, and a limited amount of information on children's story books and postcards relating to famous doll houses and various holidays. While a great number of the above paper toys are pictured and discussed, we wonder about the ones we have missed. We have no idea in what volume these paper toys were published or in how many languages they were printed. We have seen a few examples printed in German and French.

We have not included information on the many thousands of postcards Tuck produced other than the few dozen mentioned above. No mention is made of the vast assortment of art prints and paper novelties that the Tuck firm published over the years.

Marian B. Howard, in her book *Those Fascinating Paper Dolls*, wrote about the problems of researching Raphael Tuck & Sons, Ltd. She wrote, "Attempting to compile a comprehensive history of paper dolls of Raphael Tuck & Sons Ltd., poses baffling problems. Duplication of certain dolls in different series, lack of identification on both dolls and containers in many instances and other lapses, cause much confusion. It might be well to add that no assistance could be expected from the Tuck firm regarding dolls published before 1900 as their early records were destroyed during bombing raids in World War II. Thus the early dolls in today's collections are the sole remaining record of the initial production of Raphael Tuck & Sons Ltd., treasures to be preserved."

Suggested Structure For Dating the Objects of Raphael Tuck & Sons, Ltd. Queen Victoria through King George VI

The year 1866 was the start of what was to become the firm of Raphael Tuck & Sons, Ltd. To date each item precisely to the year is almost impossible. The Tuck firm was very generous in its markings on each of its published objects. Each part and each envelope or box cover was usually marked in some way. These markings or imprints established a time frame based on the length of the reign of each ruler.

1880 Tuck adapted the "Easel and Palette" trademark with the slogan, "The World's Art Service."

1881 The firm became Raphael Tuck & Sons.

1893-1901 During Queen Victoria's reign, the imprints read: "London, Paris, New York." "Published by Appointment to Her Majesty the Queen." "Publishers by Royal Warrant to..." "Publishers by Special Appointment to ..."

1895 The firm became Raphael Tuck & Sons, Ltd.

1901-1910 During King Edward VII's reign, the imprints read: "London, Paris, New York" or "London, Paris, Berlin, New York and Montreal." "Publishers to Their Majesties the King and Queen Alexandra." "Publishers to Their Majesties the King and Queen." "Publishers to Their Majesties the King and Queen and to TRH the Prince and Princess of Wales." (The Prince and Princess were Edward's son, George, and Princess Mary.) They were married in July 1893.

1907-1913 The Montreal office of the Tuck firm existed.

1907-1915 The Berlin office of the Tuck firm existed.

1910-1915 Reign of George V and Queen Mary. Imprints read: "London, Paris, Berlin, New York, Montreal." "To Their Majesties the King and Queen and H.M. Alexandra."

1913-1925 Reign of George V and Queen Mary. Imprints read: "London, Paris, New York." "To Their Majesties the King and Queen and H.M. Queen Alexandra." Alexandra died in 1925.

1925-1936 Reign of George V and Queen Mary. Imprint read: "London, Paris, New York." "To Their Majesties the King and Queen." George V died in 1936.

1936-late 1940s Reign of George VI and Queen Elizabeth. Imprint read: "London, New York and Toronto." "The King and Queen and H.M. Queen Mary," or "Her Majesty Queen Mary."

Late 1940s-1951 Reign of George VI and Queen Elizabeth. Imprint read: "London, and Northampton, New York and Toronto." "The King and Queen and to H.M. Queen Mary" or "Her Majesty Queen Mary." Queen Mary died in 1953, one year after her granddaughter, Elizabeth, became queen.

Information from Canada as to dates of the Raphael Tuck & Sons Co., Ltd., bearing the imprint "Toronto" have been inconclusive. According to the Metropolitan Toronto Reference Library, Raphael Tuck & Sons first appeared in *Might's Toronto City Directory* in 1912. The last entry in the *Toronto City Directory* was 1914 (no doubt because of the war). They also searched 1938-1950, but found nothing in Toronto directories, although Raphael Tuck & Sons Canada Limited was incorporated by the Government of Canada on June 20, 1947.

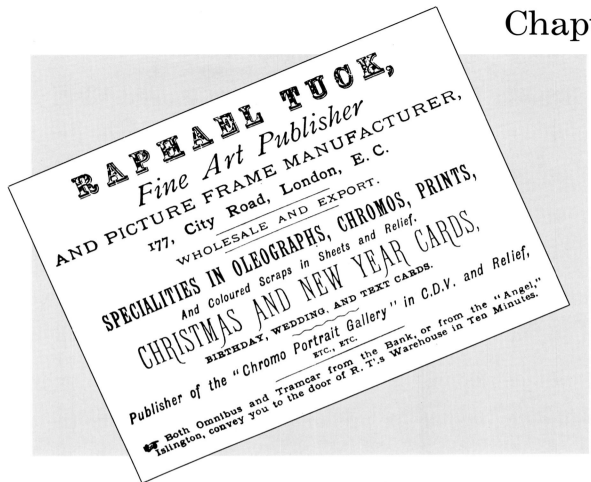

Part I
The Reign of Queen Victoria
The Early Years and Growth of a Great Publishing Company

This is a brief history of the early period of a world renowned publishing company, Raphael Tuck & Sons, Ltd., which was established in 1866 by Raphael Tuck. Our daughter, Barbara Whitton Berger, published a book on this subject in 1970. Since that time, there has been some new information in magazine articles but not an indepth study made of this company. We hope to remedy this.

Raphael Tuck was born in Koschmin, a small village in East Prussia, on August 7, 1821. In 1848, at the age of 27, he married Ernestine Lissner. In 1859, Raphael, Ernestine and their six children moved to Breslau, where Tuck felt he might have more success at earning a living for his family. It was here that their seventh child was born, forming a family of four sons and three daughters. Five years later their lives were interrupted by the Prusso-Danish and Austrian War and Raphael Tuck and his wife decided to make a move. Mr. Tuck traveled to London in 1865, found work and established living quarters for his family, who soon joined him.

Like many other men who have built the groundwork for a great and profitable business, Raphael Tuck did not start in the work which was to become his destiny. After a few unsatisfactory ventures, he and Ernestine opened a small shop selling prints and frames on what was known as Union Street, later changed to Brushfield Street in Bishopsgate.

Illustration 1. A Raphael Tuck advertisement of the 1870s. The reverse side of this card pictures a full-color print of roses. Notice in the small print it mentions: "Coloured Scraps in Sheets and Relief." Size of card is unknown.

Illustration 2. A strip of European Santa Claus scrap from a sheet published by Raphael Tuck. Marked: "Gigantic Relief No. 1345, Raphael Tuck & Sons Ltd." These figures average 4½in (11cm) in height.

The year 1866 was the start of what was to become the firm of Raphael Tuck & Sons, Ltd. The small shop soon became a thriving enterprise. Ernestine proved to be a fine business woman, a natural organizer and administrator, while Tuck himself was very creative and a perfectionist. This insistence upon perfection by Raphael Tuck was carried on by his sons through the later years and is why the firm has and is now held in high esteem in the publishing world.

Three years after opening the original shop, the business was moved to larger quarters at 177 City Road. At this point Tuck's sons, Herman, Adolph and Gustave, joined their parents in the business. From the original selling and framing of prints, the company started publishing lithographs, chromolithographs and various printed novelties.

By 1870, the three young sons were making contributions to the growth and progress of the business. Adolph worked with his father and developed similar business traits and the same level of perfectionism. Herman and Gustave became salesmen, strongly encouraged by their mother who it was said had them compare sales notes at the end of each day. **Illustration 1** pictures a Tuck advertisement of the 1870s while the reverse side carried a full-color reproduction of beautiful roses. As you can see from the advertisement, the sheets of die-cut, embossed and highly-colored scrap appeared as part of the firm's output. The scrap offered a great variety of subjects such as fairy tales, comic characters, famous people, children, animals, flowers, soldiers, fire fighters and holiday subjects. All were popular. **(Illustration 2.)** Special moments in life such as births, christenings, first loves, marriage, anniversaries and mourning were available. **(Illustration 3.)** An outstanding example of Tuck scrap is pictured in **Color Illustration 1**. The appeal of pasting bits of scrap into books was developed by young ladies into an art form. Adult handwork in scrapbooks was recognizable by some of the watercolor backgrounds of some of the creative scenes. In this same time period, children found extreme pleasure in developing scrapbooks and they also found much delight in trading bits of scrap, always looking for a piece they did not have. Interest declined slowly from 1900 until about 1940 as a variety of other time-consuming hobbies appeared and offered competition to the scrap collecting. Raphael Tuck produced a great variety of colorful scrap, the majority in the form of single sheets and others in boxed set. A further scrap item is titled "The Dancers." **(Illustration 4.)** Other scrap items that Tuck published were in the form of panoramas. An outstanding example of this form was labeled: "Father Tuck's Panorama Series" which included "Little Snow-White," "Robinson Crusoe," "Cinderella," "Feathered Friends," "Buttercup Farm," "Beauty and the Beast," "Little Red Riding Hood" and "Old Mother

Hubbard." **(Illustration 5.)** Each of these small six-section panoramas are equipped with a four-page story of the character and instructions for separating the figures and putting them on stands. The small round stands are partially die-cut on a page of heavy green stock included in the booklet. "John Gilpin" and "A Visit to the Aquarium" are two further examples. **(Illustration 6.)** It is quite possible that those pictured are but a few of Raphael Tuck's total panorama production. A further scrap item, in the form of a paper doll, appears to be not quite as common. **(Illustration 7.)**

In 1871, Raphael Tuck published his first Christmas cards. Each year their popularity increased with the public and by 1880, young Adolph Tuck instituted a nationwide competition to create newly designed Christmas cards. Raphael Tuck & Sons offered prize money totaling 500 guineas, equal to about $10,000. Five thousand paintings and designs were submitted and were judged by several eminent members of the Royal Academy. An exhibition was held in the Dudley Galleries in Piccadilly, London. The overwhelming success of the art contest and the exhibition was given press coverage by the London news media plus coverage in the larger newspapers throughout the world. The name of Raphael Tuck became known "world-wide" overnight. Collectors and historians of the development of the Christmas card recognized that these two events organized by Adolph Tuck were a turning point in the progress of Christmas cards. Christmas cards became the accepted way of expressing sentiment and goodwill at Christmas time.

In 1880, the Tuck firm registered its world famous trademark, the "Easel and Palette" with the inscription "The Worlds Art Service." A hand-written note sent from Raphael Tuck to agents who registered trademarks read: "Dear Sirs, I enclose specimen of my design which I wish registered. My firm will trade under the name

Illustration 3. A fine example of a rather large piece of scrap picturing the head and shoulders of a lovely young girl while above she is pictured as an angel playing a lyre harp. Notice the tab on upper left wing marked with the easel and palette trademark. This section of scrap measures 9½in high and 6½in wide (24 x 17cm).

Illustration 4. "The Dancers." A grouping of three different strips of scrap published by Raphael Tuck & Sons, Ltd. Dancers average 2⅝in (7cm) in height.

Illustration 5. Two six-section folded scrap panoramas titled "Cinderella" and "Robinson Crusoe." The folded panorama includes four pages of story text and a green stock page of die-cut round stands. Both panoramas are marked with their titles and "Father Tuck's Panorama Series" on the front covers. Inside they are marked with the easel and palette trademark and "Raphael Tuck & Sons Ltd, London, Paris, New York. Designed in England, Printed in Bavaria" and "No. 7004" and "7002." Folded, the panorama is 4¾in high and 3in wide (10cm x 8cm). It opens to 17¾in (45cm).

Illustration 6. "John Gilpin" and "A Visit to the Aquarium" are two further examples of scrap panoramas. The six-section John Gilpin panorama pictures Gilpin mounting a horse and the wild and exciting ride that followed. "A Visit to the Aquarium" is a six-section panorama picturing people looking down into pools containing underwater life. Both are marked: "Raphael Tuck & Sons, London, Paris, New York." Each measures 4⅝in high and 3in wide (12cm x 8cm), extended 18in (46cm).

Illustration 8. Two books from Father Tuck's "Nursery Series." Both are marked: "Painting Copyright 1895 by Raphael Tuck & Sons, London, Paris, New York, Publishers to Her Majesty the Queen." Little Red Riding Hood is marked: "No. 1477, Printed in Bavaria," while Beauty and the Beast is marked: "No. 1481, Printed in Saxony." Both books measure 10¾in high by 8½in wide (27cm x 22cm).

of Raphael Tuck & Sons from January 1st, 1881. The classes I intend to use the design for comprise of pictures of all kinds, Christmas, New Year and other congratulatory cards."

Possibly, mention should be made at this time of the fine assortment of colorful juvenile picture and shape books published by the Tuck firm. There were doubtless countless numbers published and while the subject of children's books will not be covered in detail, examples of some of them will be mentioned and appear in photographs throughout the various periods of the growth of the Tuck company. May it be noted here that some of the books were published specifically for the American market. These were marked: "New York, London, Paris." Also note that many of the books were not marked as to the current ruler of the period when they were published.

Two beautiful shape books, *Our Little Favorite* and *Our Pets* were published in London during Queen Victoria's reign. **(Color Illustration II.)** Color Illustration III pictures *Your Dolly* and *From Southern Shores*. Both of these books are from the Queen Victoria period. Other examples of colorful story books are the old-time favorites *Little Red Riding Hood* and *Beauty and the Beast*. **(Illustration 8.)** *Dog and Cat Land* and *Mother Goose* are two other examples of Tuck's works. **(Illustration 9.)** Another group of three small shape books, *A Hamper of Mischief, Dear Old Santa Claus* and *My Dolly's House* are pictured in **Illustration 18**.

A wonderful hardcover book titled *Something to Tell You* consists of several short stories by such authors as Nora Hopper, E. Rowley Watson and Anthony Guest. There are six very appealing full-page color illustrations of children by Frances Brundage and an equally talented artist by the name of M. Bowley. The cover illustration pictured is the work of Frances Brundage. **(Color Illustration IV.)** Two other books in the form of three double pop-up folding panoramas are titled *A Day in the Forest* and *The Doll's House*. The cover of the first book listed is pictured in **Color Illustration II**. The three double-spread pop-up pictures a group of six young children enjoying a picnic lunch in a wooded area when they are approached by a group of inquisitive deer. The second double illustration pictures the children and their dogs playing hide-and-seek. The final double-spread pop-up pictures some of the children picking blackberries while the others hide behind

Illustration 9. Dog and Cat Land, *No. 5554 is from the Father Tuck's "Useful Knowledge Series" and was published during King Edward's reign.* Mother Goose, *No. 1460 is from Father Tuck's "Little Pets Series" published during Queen Victoria's reign. Both are marked: "Published by Raphael Tuck & Son Co., Ltd., New York — London — Paris. Designed at the Studios in England." Both carry the easel and palette trademark. They both measure 8¾in high and 7in wide (22cm x 18cm).*

shrubbery watching a family of wild rabbits playing in an open area. The second is titled *The Dolls' House*. **(Illustration 12.)** It contains six individual pop-ups featuring children and dolls in various rooms of a house, engaging in everyday activities.

While not going into detail regarding the books published by Raphael Tuck & Sons, the variety must have been rather extensive. We have seen many examples from a variety of series over the years, each series having six or more titles. Examples observed include the following: Father Tuck's Animal Friends Series, Fairy Tale Series, Play and Pleasure Series, Little Darling Series, Little Lesson Series, Golden Gift Series, Doll Series, Christmas Series and Land and Sea Series.

Reverting back to the history of the firm, we find that Raphael Tuck had remained active in the business until 1881. At that time, he decided to retire from the firm and enjoy a well-deserved rest with his wife, Ernestine. At this time, Adolph, Herman and Gustave entered into a partnership and the name of the firm was changed to Raphael Tuck & Sons. A move was made to larger premises at Coleman Street in the city of London and to a branch building on Chiswell St. Adolph Tuck, being a very active businessman, was not content with his earlier achievement in the field of competitions and exhibitions. He forged ahead, looking for new artists and writers who would supply new ideas for the company. He organized another competition in an attempt to induce amateur writers and painters to enter their work. Four thousand prizes, in the form of money and judges' diplomas were offered to winners in various classifications open to adults. A special section was open to children of various ages. **(Illustration 13.)** Judging for this competition was done by eminent members of the Royal Academy. This included Sir John Millair, R.A., Marcus Stone, R.A., G. Boughton, R.A. and Solomon J. Solomon, A.R.A. Approximately 10,000 entries were submitted and 2500 of these were hung in a very successful exhibition in the Galleries of the Royal Institute of Painters in Water Colors in London. Adolph Tuck not only planned and executed the above mentioned contest and exhibition, but he approached other ventures. It is said that he offered the Poet Laureate, Lord Tennyson, 1000 guineas for 12 verses of eight lines each. Lord Tennyson, who was 80 years old and in poor health, refused with regret what he felt was a great opportunity.

Illustration 10. A group of three small shape books, A Hamper of Mischief, Dear Old Santa Claus and My Dolly's House. All are marked with the easel and palette trademark. They are also marked: "Artistic Series 821, 825 and 827 Raphael Tuck & Sons, London, Paris, New York. Designed at the Studios in England and Printed at the Fine Art Works in Germany." Notice these are not marked as to ruler. Average size is 5½in high and 4in wide (14cm x 10cm).

Illustration 11. The cover of "A Day in the Forest," a book-like folding panorama containing three double-page pop-ups. Marked: "Painting copyright 1895 by Raphael Tuck & Sons, London — Paris — New York. Publishers to Her Majesty the Queen." It is also marked with the easel and palette trademark, "No. 1506" and "Printed in Bavaria." The cover measures 7½in high and 9¼in wide (19 x 24cm). Extended, the panorama measures 55½in (140cm).

Illustration 12. The cover of a book-like pan-orama titled "The Dolls' House." Similar in style and construction to "A Day in the Forest," it has the same markings with the additional markings, "Designed at the Studios in England and Printed at the Fine Art Works in Bavaria." Cover measurements are the same.

Illustration 14. Raphael House, the home of Raphael Tuck & Sons' business. This opened on July 6, 1899. Raphael Tuck had laid the cornerstone the year before on April 4th.

Illustration 13. Tuck's official announcement of its "Amateurs' Literary and Painting Competition." The fine print at the bottom lists nine reviews by prominent newspapers concerning the forthcoming competition. In essence, they praise the firm of Messrs. Raphael Tuck & Sons as "Patrons of Art" in Great Britain because they encourage amateurs to participate. The size of the announcement is unknown.

By Special Appointment, Publishers to the Queen.

UPWARDS OF 4,000 PRIZES, OF THE VALUE OF

3,000 GUINEAS,

AND A NUMBER OF JUDGES' DIPLOMAS,

WILL BE AWARDED IN CONNECTION WITH

Messrs. Raphael Tuck & Sons'

NEXT

Amateurs' "Literary" and "Painting"

PRIZE COMPETITION,

(A Special Section being reserved for Children of varying ages),

IN MAY, 1895.

PRESIDENTS OF THE TWO COMMITTEES OF JUDGES:

WALTER BESANT AND MARCUS STONE, R.A.

NO ENTRANCE FEES.

Prospectus free at all leading Stationers, Booksellers, and Art Stores; where not procurable, it will be sent post free on application to

MESSRS. RAPHAEL TUCK & SONS, FINE ART PUBLISHERS,
72/73, COLEMAN STREET, CITY, LONDON.

14

In the 1880s and 1890s, the House of Tuck continued to flourish. Branches were opened in Paris and New York. In 1893, the company was granted the Royal Warrant of Appointment by Queen Victoria in recognition of its successful publication of the Queen's letter to the nation on the death of the Duke of Clarence. Each succeeding reign has so honored the House of Tuck.

At this point, we might turn away from the firm's history to try and date the many items published by them. To date each item precisely to the year is almost impossible. Company records were destroyed during bombing raids in World War II. The Tuck firm was both meticulous and generous in its markings on each of its published items. Each separate part and each envelope or box cover which was published was marked in some way. These markings or imprints established a time frame based on the length of the reign of each ruler rather than to a specific year. From 1893 until 1901, when Queen Victoria died, the imprint read as follows: "Published by Appointment to Her Majesty, the Queen." Sometimes the phrase read: "Publishers by Special Appointment to --," "publishers by Royal Warrant to --" or similar wording. Only the ruler's identification is important to the time frame.

From 1901-1910, during the reign of Edward VII and Queen Alexandra, the line read: "Their Majesties the King and Queen" or "Their Majesties the King and Queen and TRH the Prince and Princess of Wales" (George and Mary). From 1910-1925, during the reign of George V and Queen Mary, it read: "Their Majesties the King and Queen and H.M. Alexandra." From 1925-1936, during the reign of George V and Queen Mary, it read: "To Their Majesties the King and Queen." From 1936 to 1952, during the reign of George VI and Queen Elizabeth, it read: "The King and Queen and to H.M. Queen Mary or Her Majesty Queen Mary."

In addition to the Royal Appointments and a few patent dates, either English or American, an imprint named the cities in which Raphael Tuck & Sons had branch offices. Early on, it listed London, Paris and New York. Later listings were London, Paris, Berlin, New York and Montreal. Those objects which include the marking "Montreal" were published between 1907 and 1913. The Montreal City Directories, for the period 1907-1913, carried the following listing: "Raphael Tuck & Sons Co. Ltd. 9-17 St Antoine Street, Christmas cards, calendars, toy books and post card publishers."

While the above-mentioned imprints do not mention a specific year, they do offer a range of years. The imprint also offered information as to where the printing was done. Many items are marked: "Designed at the Studios in England, Printed at the Fine Art Works in Saxony," "Designed at the Studios in New York and Printed at the Fine Art Works in Bavaria" or simply "Printed in Germany."

Illustration 15. *The decorative front and back covers of an 1885 Tuck catalog issued from the New York City branch at 298 Broadway. The 54-page wholesale catalog measures 9¼in high and 8⅛in wide (24cm x 21cm).*

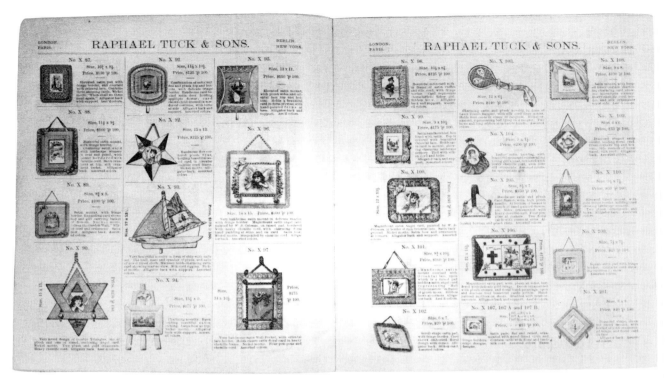

Illustration 16. A double-page spread of hanging Christmas and New Year novelties pictured in the 1885 Tuck catalog issued from the New York City office.

In 1885, Ernestine Tuck died and much credit should be given to her dedication to the firm. It had reached a high level of endeavor and activity. During this year, Raphael Tuck & Sons was formed into a private limited company. Adolph Tuck became managing director with his brothers, Herman and Gustave, as co-directors. The firm's capital amounted to 110,000 pounds with debitures of 30,000 pounds. The whole of the former and the majority of the latter amount was taken up by Adolph, Herman and Gustave and the remainder by their brother, Hugo, a few other relatives and some employees.

After the death of Ernestine, Raphael Tuck's health began to fail. On April 4, 1898, he laid the foundation stone for a magnificent new office building. It was constructed to house all the activities of the firm he and Ernestine had founded. It was located in an area called Moorfields and from its roof you could view the city of London. The new building was named Raphael House and it was formally opened on July 6, 1899. **(Illustration 14.)** In March of the following year, Raphael Tuck passed away in the presence of his family. He was 79 years old.

In mentioning the growth and progress of the Tuck company, mention should be made of one of the catalogs. An 1885 Tuck catalog, issued from the New York office at 298 Broadway, gives us an idea of the variety of products offered during this period of time. **(Illustration 15.)** This wholesale catalog of 54 pages lists, and in some cases, illustrates items offered to the trade. Unfortunately, there is only one page of paper toys, paper dolls and other juvenile items. A brief summary of the contents is as follows: the first six pages carry an extensive listing of artistic prints. This is followed by six pages of hanging Christmas and New Year novelties in various shapes. They range in size from 5in x 6in (13cm x 15cm) to 14in x 15in (36cm x 38cm). Nearly all are enclosed on a satin-covered mount or frame. Many have an outer edge trimmed with fringe. **(Illustration 16.)** This is followed by several pages listing a variety of floral prints, then eight pages of assorted birthday cards, script cards and wedding cards. The next three pages picture an Artistic Line of four cent scrap sheets. Only one page lists items of interest to children. **(Illustration 17.)** Following this page there are illustrated and embossed papier-mâché plaques in three sizes, artistically decorated fans and a wide selection of folding screens. The last few pages provide a listing of fine Oleographs which are reproductions of works of art by such artists as Rubens, Rembrandt, Erelman, Franz Meerts, Burgers, and so forth. These reproductions are processed by the celebrated "Peinture-Bogaerts process which makes it impossible even for connoisseurs to distinguish them from originals." The quote goes on to say "Every tint, every line, shade, every line of the brush and application of the paint can be distinctly seen. The canvas, the texture, all are clearly reproduced."

16

RAPHAEL TUCK & SONS'
ARTISTIC NOTIONS AND NOVELTIES.
—◆ JUST ISSUED. ◆—

EMBOSSED PICTURES, (on 8 x 10 Mounts).

Something Entirely New!

Put up in neat boxes, each containing 100 Assorted Pictures, no two alike, of Birds, Animals, Flowers, Fruit, Landscapes, Figures, etc.

Price per Box of 100 Pictures, $3.25.

THE NEW PAINTING BOOK,
FOR BOYS AND GIRLS.

Containing 16 colored models, and 16 outlines for painting. Size of Book, 4 x 5½. An endless source of pleasure and instruction for the young. Put up in Boxes, each containing 50 Books, at $1.50 per Box.

EXCELSIOR PICTURE FRAMES.

Designed for both single and double Carte de Visite pictures. Made of superior bristol, upon which very choice sprays and garlands of flowers are printed and embossed, encircling the picture. Substantial slide and back, also support to stand. 8 assorted patterns, put up in boxes, each containing 50 frames.

Price of Single Frames, size, $2.00 per box of 50.
" Double " size, $4.00 " "

Besides being a pretty ornament for mantel, etc., they are most popular with photographers, who in delivering their pictures in these frames, easily realize cost, and profit.

DECALCOMANIE PICTURES.

A large variety of colored pictures, which by using a little water, will transfer on to china, glass, scrap-books, etc. Amusing to children, also useful in ornamenting household articles of every description.

Put up in Boxes of 25 sheets, assorted Flowers, Animals, Soldiers, Landscapes, etc. Each Box containing nearly 1,000 distinct pictures.

Size, 7¼ x 6. Price, $1 per Box.

"HAPPY HOURS."—A.

A fancy ornamented Box of large Scrap Pictures, containing a variety of 50 sheets of Heads, Figures and Flowers, etc., no two alike. Size, 7 x 5¼. Price, $1.25.

"HAPPY HOURS."—B.

A beautiful ornamented Box containing 100 sheets Scrap Pictures, giving one sheet each of our principal styles, no two sheets alike. The size is 6 x 8. Price, $2.50.

TOY BOOKS.

Our line of Toy Books which we offer to the Trade, are, far superior to any similar productions of this market. Printed from stone, in the very best manner, and from designs of eminent *Artists*. Printed clearly.—Yes! even elegantly, on superior heavy paper, and no expense spared to make them good and attractive. Each book contains 32 pages, 8 full page *colored* plates, and innumerable designs, in one color.

Size, 8 x 9½. Price $30 per 100 Books.

We have three series:
"DARLINGS A. B. C."
"ADVENTURES OF VALENTINE PIMPLE."
"HAIL COLUMBIA."

VELOUTINE.

The Veloutine Painting Medium for Oil and Water Colors.

The newly perfected Veloutine entirely supersedes the various special *media* hitherto in use by artists and amateurs for painting, on such ground or material which has a tendency to the spreading of colors, and as now prepared, is equally applicable to either oil or water colors, and to the entire range of textile fabrics, china, glass, terra cotta, leather, cloth, etc. This medium has additional advantage of imparting softness and brilliancy to the colors.

☞ Full Directions for Use Accompany Every Bottle. ☜

Small Bottles. $60 per 100.
Large " $90 "

Illustration 17. The one page in the 1885 catalog that offers toys. A panorama type "New Painting Book" that contains a top row of 16 colored models and a lower row of 16 outlines to paint in. "Decalcomanie Pictures" containing a variety of colored pictures which with the use of a little water may be transferred onto china, glass or paper. "Happy Hours A or B," a box containing 50 assorted sheets of scrap and lastly, some toy books.

Illustration 18. A wonderful example of an educational book for young children. Father Tuck's ABC Spelling Book was issued as part of Father Tuck's "Little Lesson Series." The book is marked with the easel and palette trademark and "No. 2077." Printed markings are as follows: "Raphael Tuck & Sons Ltd., London, Paris, New York, Publishers to the Queen, Designed in England, Printed in Bavaria." Size, 8in high by 11½in wide (20cm x 29cm)

17

Included in the "Notes" at the end of the catalog is the statement, "Orders for any part of the United States, Canada and Canadian Provinces, Mexico, West India Islands and all of South American countries will be filled from our New York Branch, who are destined to control the entire American market. When the order warrants, we will ship from London or from Hamburg, and make reasonable allowance for American duties which we save by shipping from foreign ports."

Turning back to the continuing story of the House of Tuck, one department after another became part of the Tuck pattern. In addition to the increased production of greeting and holiday cards, a variety of attractive calendars and children's books appeared, books designed not only to offer pleasure to the young, but to instruct. **(Illustration 18.)**

Father Tuck's ABC Spelling Book contains several pages of line drawings of animals and birds. However, the big surprise is two double-page spreads in brilliant color, one with a strip of pop-up cutout dogs and cats, the other with a strip of pop-up boys and girls. As the book opens out to a 22¾in (58cm) spread, the six figures on each double spread are very impressionable. **(Color Illustration V.)** Beautifully illustrated children's stories were published in the form of colorful picture books, shape books and movable books. **(Illustration 19.)**

In his pioneering of fine art publishing, Adolph Tuck gave much attention to pictorial postcards. The various series, published under the title "Oilette," are considered highly collectible in the United States. Tuck's first pictorial postcard was published as an experiment in 1894. The card featured, in the top left corner, a small picture of the Welsh mountain Snowdon. The reason for the small corner picture was that it was compulsory for one side of the postcard to be devoted to the address and the reverse side to the message. The maximum length of the card was limited to 3½in (9cm). Adolph Tuck negotiated with the Postmaster General in an attempt to change this form of the postcard. After four years of meetings, the Postmaster General finally agreed to a change in the format and size of postcards. This resulted in the eventual emergence of what became a new industry. This industry produced local view postcards and pictorial cards of various other subjects of public interest. Adolph Tuck realized the potential of these picture postcards. Within a few years, worldwide pictorial postcard collector clubs were organized. Membership was open to all who bought and traded Tuck postcards. By 1900, the Tuck company was publishing nearly 40,000 different pictorial postcards.

Illustration 19. A shape book of Father Christmas handing a doll to a little girl. It is titled A Letter From Old Father Christmas by E. Lecky with illustrations by Emily J. Harding. Marked with the Tuck trademark and the words, "Raphael Tuck & Sons, London, Paris, New York. Designed at the London Studios and printed at the Fine Art Works in Bavaria." 9¾in high by 6⅝in wide (25cm x 17cm).

OPPOSITE PAGE: Color Illustration I. *A complete set of 15 scrap squares including a title square and a table of contents square which act as covers for the 13 fragile squares illustrating the past rulers of Britain. Titled "Kings & Queens of England, The Entire Series of 37 rulers from William the Conqueror to Queen Victoria." Title square marked: "Raphael Tuck & Sons, London, New York, Paris, Berlin." Each square measures 4⅝in high by 5¾in wide (12cm x 15cm).*

THE KINGS AND QUEENS OF ENGLAND
From WILLIAM the CONQUEROR to Queen VICTORIA

THE ENTIRE SERIES OF 37 RULERS
TOGETHER WITH THE GREAT SEAL AND COIN OF EACH RESPECTIVE REIGN

COMPRISED IN 13 SHEETS OF RELIEFS

PRICE ONE SHILLING

RAPHAEL TUCK & SONS
FINE ART PUBLISHERS

Contents.

Color Illustration II. *Our Little Favourite and Our Pets, two lovely shape books. Dainty ten-page booklets filled with verses and illustrations of children and their pet animals. Both are marked with the Tuck trademark and "No. 1456" and "1458," and "Raphael Tuck & Sons, London, Paris, New York, Publishers to the Queen, Painting Copyright 1895, Printed in Saxony." Both books measure 9¾in high by 5in wide (25cm x 13cm).*

Color Illustration III. *Two interesting shape books, Your Dolly, No. 2025 and From Southern Shores, No. 1447. Your Dolly published for the American market is marked: "Raphael Tuck & Sons Co., Ltd., New York-London-Paris, Designed at the Studios in England." From Southern Shores is marked: "Painting Copyrighted 1895 by Raphael Tuck & Sons, London, Paris, New York, Publishers to the Queen, Printed at the Fine Art Works in Germany." Your Dolly measures 9⅝in high and 5⅛in wide (24cm x 13cm). From Southern Shores is 9in high and 4⅛in wide (23cm x 11cm).*

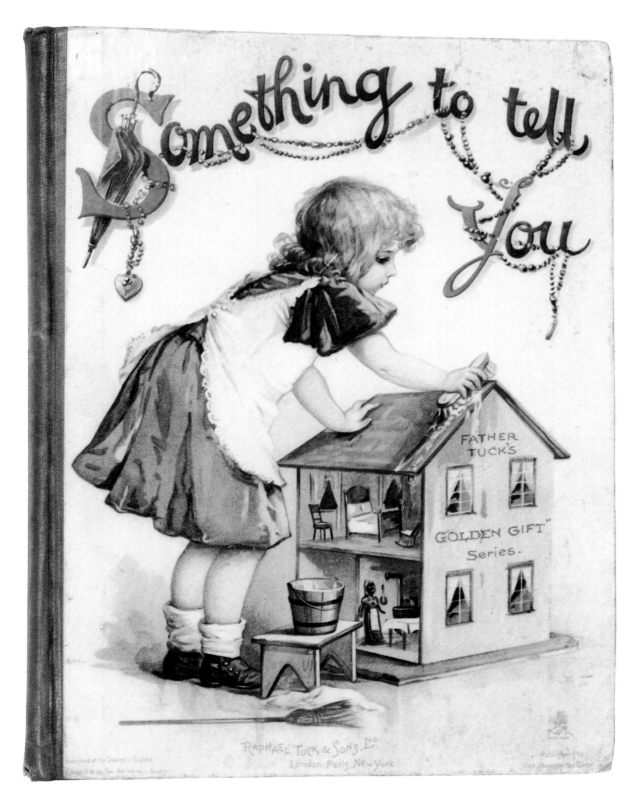

Color Illustration IV. *A hard cover 63-page book from the "Golden Gift Series," titled* Something to Tell You. *It contains several short stories with color illustrations by F. Brundage and M. Bowley. The book is marked with the easel and palette trademark and "Raphael Tuck & Sons Ltd., London, Paris, New York, Publishers to Her Majesty the Queen, Designed at the Studios in England and Printed at the Fine Art Works in Saxony." The book measures 10in high by 7½in wide (25cm x 19cm).*

Color Illustration V. One of the double-page pop-ups picturing three dogs and three cats standing on their hind legs. This is one of two fabulous pop-ups in Father Tuck's ABC Spelling Book. *The animals stand 6in (15cm) high and the six spread out 20in (51cm).*

Color Illustration VI. The contents of the boxed set "For Queen and Country" consisting of representatives of six regiments of British Cavalry. The back of each cavalryman carries the name of the regiment he represents and the easel and palette trademark. There is also the wording: "By Special Appointment, Publishers to Her Majesty the Queen, Raphael Tuck & Sons, London, Paris, New York, Designed at the Studios in England, Printed at the Fine Art Works in Saxony, Copyright, Royal Art Series 141." Mounted soldiers stand 10in (25cm) tall.

Chapter I

Part II

Those Intriguing Early Paper Toys
During the Reign of Queen Victoria

During Queen Victoria's reign, the firm of Raphael Tuck & Sons published a variety of beautiful and unusual paper toys. Most of these toys were highly colored, die-cut in form and many were embossed. All were of high quality. **Illustration 20** pictures a charming set of fragile figures featuring children and their pets. These two-piece figures are hinged so that they may be spread and made to stand upright. The little girl is in the land of make believe; her chair is her horse. On the back of the figure is the title "A Safe Gallop." The baby is enjoying the play between the cat and her kitten. It is titled "Nursery Playmates." The boy, teasing his pet dog, is titled "Good Doggie." The child and mother say the "Evening Prayer" while "The Little Mariner" readies his boat for a sail.

Illustration 21 pictures a boxed set titled "Driving to Pasture." This contains six child figures, each with a grouping of farm animals or bird friends. **Illustration 22** pictures the "Young Riders" from the Artistic Toy Novelty Series, No. 122. It shows the original box cover and its rather well-played-with contents, two horses and six youthful riders. All are brilliantly colored, die-cut and embossed. The backs of the riders are equipped with a slip-on tab so that the riders may be positioned on the backs of the horses.

A blue box titled "Rocking Horses" with a subtitle "Artistic Toy Novelty Series No. 120," contains five colorful die-cut young people, each riding a dapple gray rocking horse. A sixth figure represents a black youth riding on the back of a black clown who is positioned on a pair of rockers. Each of the six figures has a rear rocker

Illustration 20. A whimsical set of fragile die-cut figures featuring happy children and their playful pets. The back of each figure is marked with an appropriate title and the easel and palette trademark, "London, Paris, New York, Publishers to Her Majesty the Queen" and "Designed at the Studios in England and Printed at the Fine Art Works in Germany." The figures average 6½in (17cm) in height.

Illustration 21. *"Driving to Pasture" is a lovely boxed set containing six figures, each tending a group of farm fowl or animals. It is marked: "Artistic Toy Novelty Series No. 123, Publishers to the Queen, London, Paris, New York." The box measurements are 6in high, 5¼in wide and ⅝in deep (15cm x 13cm x 2cm). The standing colorful embossed groups average 4½in high, 4in wide and 1½in deep (11cm x 10cm x 4cm). This set came in either a blue or tan box.*

Illustration 22. *"Young Riders" is the title on the original box containing two well-played-with horses and six youthful riders. All are brilliantly colored, die-cut and embossed. The backs of the rider figures are unmarked; horses are marked: "Artistic Toy Novelty Series No. 122, by Special Appointment Publishers to Her Majesty the Queen, London, Paris, New York." The horses stand 6½in high and are 8¾in long (17cm x 22cm). The sitting figures are 6in high (15cm).*

Illustration 23-A. Titled "Rocking Horses," this blue box is also marked: "Artistic Toy Novelty Series No. 120" and "Publishers to the Queen, London, Paris, New York." Also pictured are two of the original six rocking toys. Box size 6⅛in high, 6½in wide and ¾in deep (16cm x 17cm x 2cm).

Illustration 23-B. The remaining contents of the "Rocking Horses" set, a black girl with a doll, a boy with a horn, a soldier boy and two jolly blacks. These rocking figures stand 5in tall and are 6in wide (13cm x 15cm).

Illustration 24. A second boxed set of "Rocking Horses," identical in style to Illustration 20. This box with cover is light tan in color but is the same size and has similar markings. It is rather strange and a bit confusing that these two sets have the same No. 120. However, the six rocking figures are different, although in size they are similar to those pictured in Illustration 23-B.

Illustration 25. "See Yourself" is the title on an enveloped set containing three very colorful happy couples. One figure holds a real glass mirror while the second person poses in front of it. The figures are marked: "Publishers to the Queen, London, Paris, New York." The box cover carries the additional marking "Artistic Toy Novelty Series No. 130." These die-cut figures stand 7¾in high (20cm).

attached to the back of each horse, enabling it to stand upright and be rocked. **(Illustrations 23-A & 23-B.)** A second box set titled "Rocking Horses" is similar in size, shape and markings but is a light tan in color. The contents of this set are similar in form, yet the characters themselves are different. Three dressed animals and three human figures ride the six rocking horses. **(Illustration 24.)**

A very unusual novelty boxed set titled "See Yourself," contains three happy looking couples. In each group one figure in the rear holds a real glass mirror while the other figure peers into the mirror in a humorous manner. The figures are hinged together, giving them a means of standing upright. There is also a feeling of depth which is emphasized by the mirror. **(Illustration 25.)**

"The Flying Wonder" is a boxed set containing six attractive, youthful figures, each holding a length of thin spring-like wire. At the uppermost end of the wire is a flying paper bird, a kite or similar flying object. A slight breeze or the movement of the toy itself causes the bird, and so forth, to move back and forth in a somewhat natural manner. **(Illustration 26.)**

An interesting set, which unfortunately is incomplete and is missing its original box, is in the form of a transformation. A variety of heads are pictured, each of which may be slipped over any of the four stationary heads, changing the original character completely. This transformation toy must have given many moments of glee to its young owner over the years. Each of the four standing figures has a title on the back. Reading from left to right: "Character Sketches," "Home for the Holidays," "A Matinee" and "Jack's Benefit." **(Illustration 27.)**

The cover of a large box containing a simple, yet decorative set-up toy titled "Meadowsweet Farm" is our next toy **(Illustration 28-A)**. **Illustration 28-B** pictures the various toy parts in set-up position. The three-section background is supplemented with three smaller fold-out sections. These consist of the corncrib on the left, the extension of the house on the right and the two girls at the fence in front of it. Several die-cut domestic animals and young farm maidens are positioned throughout the scene.

Another novel paper toy published by the Tuck firm is titled "All the Fun of the Fair." The interesting yellow box cover features a line drawing of a stage and a proscenium featuring three wild animals. One animal is sitting upright playing a banjo while the other two animals stand upright, dancing on their hind legs. One holds a tambourine while the other has castanets held in his front paws. This stage setting, the title and all other printed information is done in brown ink. **Illustration 29-A** pictures the box cover along with two of the paper toys, two cage wagons marked: "The Lovely Ella" and "The Marvelous Menagerie." Action is provided by one or two horizontal pull bases that may be pulled back and forth, providing movement to the performers and/or animals which are attached to the center of

Illustration 26. "The Flying Wonder" is a boxed set containing six figures, each holding a wire which has a flying object attached to the upper end. The back of each figure has an appropriate title, the easel and palette trademark and "Raphael Tuck & Sons, London, Paris, New York. Publishers to Her Majesty the Queen, Designed at the Studios in England and Printed at the Fine Art Works in Germany." The average height of the figures is 5in (13cm). The box with cover is 7½in high, 4⅝in wide and ⅝in deep (19cm x 12cm x 2cm).

Illustration 27. *An outstanding set which is missing the original box and possibly two standing figures and possibly a head or two. However, the majority of the pieces are present and are well worth the photographic space. Each figure is marked: "Royal Art Novelty Series 142" and "Publishers to Her Majesty the Queen." The standing figures are 7⅛in tall, 5½in wide and 1in deep (18cm x 14cm x 3cm).*

Illustration 28-A. *The cover of a large box housing a simple yet decorative set-up toy titled "Meadowsweet Farm." The box and cover are rather worn but intact. It measures 12¼in high, 15⅛in wide and 1in deep (32cm x 39cm x 3cm).*

Illustration 28-B. A view of the various parts of the "Meadowsweet Farm" set up. On the back of the center background section is the printed title "Meadowsweet Farm," a listing of the set's contents, plus the Tuck trademark. The familiar "Raphael Tuck & Sons Ltd, Publishers to the Queen, London, Paris, New York" also appears. When set up, the background is 8in high, 21½in wide and 12in deep (21cm x 55cm x 31cm).

Illustration 29-A. The original yellow box cover with the dark brown printing titled "All the Fun of the Fair." It contains six traveling shows with movable figures and carries the easel and palette trademark and "No. 1468, Raphael Tuck & Sons, London, Paris, New York, Publishers to the Queen." The two cage wagons are marked: "The Lovely Ella" and "The Marvelous Menagerie" and carry the same markings as those on the box cover. The box is 5in high, 8in wide and ⅝in deep (13cm x 20cm x 2cm). The cages are 4½in high, 4¾in wide and 1in deep (11cm x 12cm x 3cm).

the pull bars. Each unit is strongly colored, embossed, die-cut and so designed that it may be opened from a flat storage position to an oblong box-like structure and made to stand upright. **Illustration 29-B** pictures the remaining four circus wagons. The "Romeo & Juliet" show is presented on an elevated stage with the two principals able to move from one side of the stage to the other. "The Happy Family" is the name given to a group of animals enclosed in a cage wagon. The "Punch & Judy" act is in the form of an upright theater in which four die-cut characters perform. They are manipulated by individual vertical shafts. It is advertised as "Punch & Judy as played before the Queen of England and the Crowned Heads of Europe, Asia, Africa & America." The fourth scene shows a group of various performers including a strongman, a juggler, an acrobat and a man performing a balancing act. This scene is titled "Walk Up! Walk Up!" The six examples are highly colorful, die-cut, embossed and amusing. This is very typical of a 19th century European traveling circus show.

Mention should be made of the paint books offered by Tuck during this early period. The few that we have observed have been rather small in size, few pages and usually have a simple one-color cover. The inside page includes a color picture on the left-hand side with a matching outline sketch on the opposite page to paint in. **Illustration 30** pictures the inside center spread of a painting book titled "The New Painting Book for Boys and Girls." This example is a far cry from the highly decorated and educational coloring books that the Tuck firm published in later years.

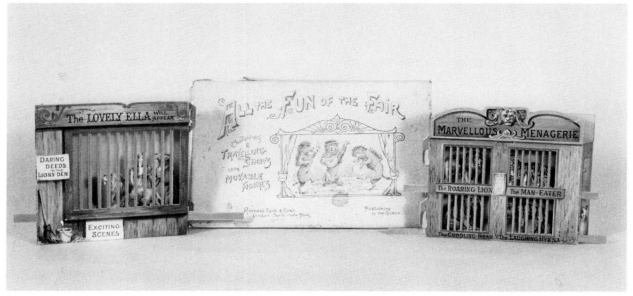

ABOVE: Illustration 29-B. The remaining four traveling shows mentioned in Illustration 29-A. They consist of a "Romeo & Juliet" show, "The Happy Family," a "Punch & Judy" show and "Walk Up! Walk Up!" Each object carries the Tuck trademark and the following lettering: "Publishers to Her Majesty the Queen, Raphael Tuck & Sons, London, Paris, New York, Designed in the Studios in England and Printed at the Fine Art Works in Germany." Average height is 4¼in by 3¾in wide by 1¾in deep (11cm x 10cm x 4cm). The "Punch & Judy" show stands 6in high, 2½in wide and 1¾in deep (15cm x 6cm x 4cm).

ABOVE: Illustration 30. The inside center spread of a small painting booklet titled "The New Painting Book for Boys and Girls." The blue covered booklet contains eight pages. Markings on the book read: "Copyright, Raphael Tuck & Sons, London" and the Tuck trademark. Measurements are 5⅛in high by 4in wide (13cm x 10cm).

LEFT: Illustration 31. This set titled "Ever New" consists of a large tan envelope that contains ten large colorful figures. It was a part of the "Artistic Toy Novelty Series No. 146." The envelope and figures are marked: "Raphael Tuck & Sons, Ltd, London, Paris, New York. Designed at the Studios in England and Printed at the Fine Art Works in Bavaria." The envelope is 14⅛in high by 8½in wide (36cm x 22cm). The figures average 13¼in high (34cm).

Illustration 32. A three-tier peep show depicting the story of Cinderella. The wide opening of the face card is unlike the usual European peep shows with the small see-through hole. The back of the rear card is marked with the Tuck trademark and the words: "Raphael Tuck & Sons, London, Paris, New York, Publishers to Her Majesty the Queen, No. 1439, Designed at the Studios in England, Printed at the Fine Art Works in Germany. Copyright." This peep show stands 6⅛in tall, 5in wide and extends 7in backwards. (16cm x 13cm x 18cm).

Illustration 33. A boxed set marked: "For Queen and Country" and "Royal Art Novelty Series No. 141." It contains six colorful examples of regiments of British Cavalry. The box is 1½in high, 4½in wide and 1⅝in deep (27cm x 11cm x 4cm).

RIGHT: *Illustration 34.* The "King's Royal Rifles" is a part of the Royal Art Novelty Series, No. 182. The row of soldiers may be folded flat or spread and be made to stand upright. Marked: "Publishers to the Queen, Raphael Tuck & Sons, London, Paris, New York." The soldiers measure 3⅞in tall (10cm). William Nutting Collection.

Illustration 35-A. *The box cover of a wonderful "Merry Go Round" toy. Actually, as it states on the cover, it is a "Capital Game and Entertaining Toy Combined." It is numbered 132 and is from the "Royal Art Novelty Series" and is patented. It is marked with the easel and palette trademark and "Publishers to the Queen, Raphael Tuck & Sons, London, Paris and New York. Invented and Designed in England, Produced in Germany." The box measures 9⅞in high, 9¾in wide and 1¼in deep (25cm x 25cm x 3cm).*

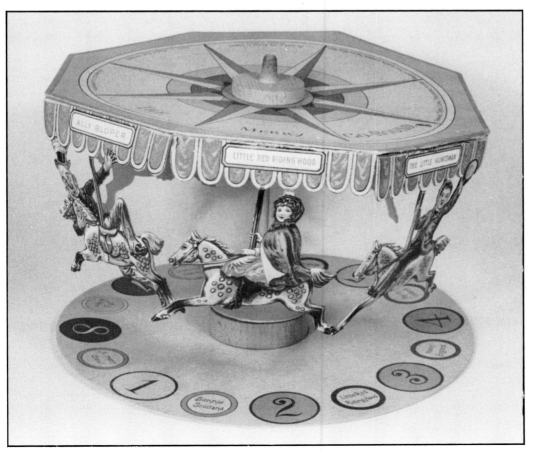

Illustration 35-B. *The "Merry Go Round" toy set up. Markings on the toy are similar to those appearing on the box. Assembled, the toy stands 6½in high and has a diameter of 8⅝in (17cm x 22cm).*

Illustration 36-A. *The box cover of the set titled "Noah's Ark Animals" and two pairs of animals, cats and lions. The cover is marked with the above title and the easel and palette trademark, also "Raphael Tuck & Sons, Publishers to the Queen, London. Paris and New York." Cover measures 8in x 10½in (20cm x 27cm). The animals are unmarked.* Maurine Popp Collection.

Illustration 36-B. *Donkeys, cows, dogs, bears, tigers, all inhabitants of Noah's Ark. All animals are unmarked and average 6in (15cm) in length.*

A set that must have brought pleasure to young boys and girls during Victoria's reign was titled "Ever New." Marked: "Artistic Toy Novelty Series No. 146," the large tan envelope contained ten large die-cut figures representing popular storybook characters. Included were colorful representations of "Dick Whittington, Babes in the Woods, Little Bo-Peep, Cinderella, Robinson Crusoe, Old Mother Hubbard, Little Boy Blue, Little Miss Muffet, The Old Woman Who Lived in a Shoe and Little Red Riding Hood." (Illustration 31.) Each figure is equipped with an attached stand, enabling the figure to stand upright.

Raphael Tuck & Sons also published its own form of a "Peep Show" during the Victorian period. An open proscenium-like front reveals "Cinderella" in her home setting being greeted by a small fairy. The second frame pictures a cut-out Prince meeting Cinderella at the ball while the rear frame pictures Cinderella being fitted with the glass slipper while her two spoiled sisters look on. The story of Cinderella in verse is printed on the back of the folded cards. (Illustration 32.)

Another example of a Tuck paper toy produced during Queen Victoria's reign is in the form of a set of magnificent soldiers on horseback. The boxed set is titled "For Queen and Country." It contains an example of six crack regiments of British

Illustration 36-C. Camels, elephants, horses, reindeer and goats are additional passengers on Noah's Ark. These animals are unmarked and average 7½in (19cm) in length.

Cavalry, "the 2nd Life Guards, Royal Horse Guards, 17th Lancers, the 11th Hussars and the Royal Scots Greys." Each cavalry officer is made up of three colorful die-cut parts, a front view of the horse, the officer astride the horse's body and the hindquarters of the horse. The three sections are joined together by two double accordion-type tabs which, when spread out, enable the horse to stand in an upright position. This set is titled the "Royal Art Novelty Series No. 141." (Illustration 33 & Color Illustration VI.)

An unusual type of paper soldier toy is next. A row of six soldiers are connected by a unique double cardboard strip running through each body. The row of soldiers may be folded flat or spread and be made to stand upright. (Illustration 34.) They are dressed in dark blue uniforms with red pin striping and decorated with blue-gray braiding. The uniforms of the "King's Royal Rifles" appears to be the title. Notice the detail in the faces; all are different and each one is in a different position. The detail is extremely fine as these figures are only 3⅞ (10cm) tall. The soldiers are die-cut, embossed and highly colored with a glossy sheen. Other British regiments represented in this "Royal Art Novelty Series, No. 182" are: "Infantry of the Line," "The Royal Engineers," "Blue Jackets of the Royal Navy," "Gordon Highlanders" and "Coldstream Guards."

Illustration 37. The tan envelope is marked: *"Artistic Toy Novelty Series No. 145, Fun on The Sands."* Companion set to the immensely successful set *"Young Riders."* Marked: *"Raphael Tuck & Sons Ltd., Publishers to the Queen, London, Paris & New York."* Included in the set are two donkeys and seven single and double riders. Each donkey and some of the riders are titled on the back, some are unmarked. Envelope measures 7⅜in x 9⅞in (19cm x 25cm). Figures vary in height from 4⅛in to 8in (11cm x 20cm).

Illustration 38-A. Box cover of the *"Healthy Pastimes"* set, marked with the easel and palette trademark and *"Artistic Toy Novelty Series No. 121, Novel Realistic Group From Life, Raphael Tuck & Sons, Publishers to the Queen, London, Paris, New York."* Cover measures 8¾in x 10¼in (22cm x 26cm).

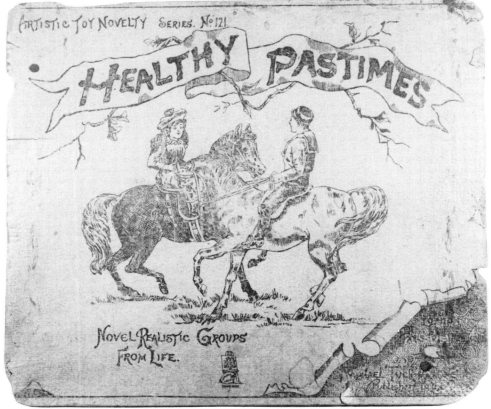

A further example of a Tuck paper toy published during the Victorian period is one in the form of a "Merry Go Round." The box cover carries that title and a colored drawing of the Merry Go Round itself. **(Illustration 35-A.)** The parts of the merry go round must be put together to form a workable toy that will spin when so desired. The toy itself consists of nine die-cut figures, seven of them riding on seven dapple gray carousel horses. The remaining two children are sitting in a face-to-face swing. All the figures are highly colored and glossy. All are hanging around the outer edge of the carousel roof. The cardboard roof and riding figures are supported by a center post in the form of a wooden dowel that is fixed to a round wood base. This base is centered on a large cardboard disc that has a number of value circles marked around the outside edge of the cardboard disc. This is both a game and a toy combined. Unfortunately, the game rules are missing. **(Illustration 35-B.)**

An interesting paper toy set titled "Noah's Ark Animals" is a set that must have delighted children of the Victorian period. It consists of an original tan box and cover marked: "Raphael Tuck & Sons, Publishers to the Queen." Contents of the box are a number of pairs of animals including the following; elephants, camels, cows, horses, dogs, cats, goats, elks, lions, tigers and donkeys. Each pair is appropriately colored, die-cut and embossed. Each pair is slightly different in the position of the legs and head. Each pair is connected by two accordion-type tabs enabling the like animals to stand side by side. This wonderful toy with a Biblical background attracts the attention of children and collectors alike. **(Illustrations 36-A, 36-B & 36-C.)**

The last two sets featured in the Victorian period concern children riding horseback. The first set is titled "Fun on the Sands." The contents include two saddled donkeys and seven slip-on riders or pairs of riders. The backs of the figures are equipped with tabs, enabling them to be slipped over the donkey's saddle. One donkey is titled "The Pride of the Beach," the other "Patient Neddy." Some of the riders are marked on the back — others are not. The large tan-colored envelope is printed with maroon ink. **(Illustration 37.)** The second set is titled "Healthy Pastimes" and includes of four double standing figures, each consisting of a walking figure leading a horse on which sits a young rider. The two pieces are connected by an accordion-type strap which enables the figures to stand side by side. The two units pictured are titled "A Ride on the Sands" on the left and "A Riding Session" on the right. **Illustration 38-A** pictures the box cover while two of the four units are seen in **Illustration 38-B**.

Illustration 38-B. Two of four units in the set titled "Healthy Pastimes." Figures are marked with a title and the easel and palette trademark. Additional printed markings are: "Publishers to Her Majesty the Queen, Raphael Tuck & Sons, London, Paris & New York, Designed at the Studios in England and Printed at the Fine Art Works in Germany." Figures stand 7¼in tall (18cm).

Chapter I

Part III

Victorian Paper Dolls and Their Fashionable Costumes During the Reign of Queen Victoria

BELOW RIGHT: Illustration 39. A copy of a portion of the British Patent No. 11367 which Adolph Tuck & Florence Prince Scott applied for on June 9, 1893.

BELOW: Illustration 40. "The Heavenly Twins" is the title of this set consisting of two baby paper dolls, one black and one white. They were based on Adolph Tuck's and Florence Prince Scott's British Patent No. 11,367 of 1893. The babies are 6in (15cm) tall. The envelope is 4in high by 6¼in wide (10cm x 16cm). Maurine Popp Collection.

The Raphael Tuck firm published the ultimate paper dolls in both artistry and magnificent color. Certainly no expense seemed to be spared in order to create the best possible results in this field. Indications are that they probably introduced their line of paper dolls in the early 1890s. No actual starting date has been found as yet, but we can determine a possible date.

The first dated paper doll published by Raphael Tuck & Sons was "The Heavenly Twins." The early paper doll researcher, Luella Hart, wrote about The Heavenly Twins in her book, *Directory of British Dolls*. This paper doll was covered by the British Patent No. 11367 and was issued to Adolph Tuck and Florence Prince Scott. Florence Scott is listed in the patent as an artist and designer. The patent was applied for on June 9, 1893, and was granted on April 14, 1894. Unlike the United States patents, the British patents become effective on the date of application, not on the date granted. **(Illustration 39.)** The specifications for this patent read in part: "According to our invention the representation of a face, say for instance a baby's face, and so much of the bust as may be intended to be seen, is printed, preferably in colours on pasteboard, or is mounted on pasteboard, or the like, and is cut out, that is to say, the superfluous material beyond the printed part is cut away leaving it in the shape of a head. The hands and part of the arms are treated in a like manner and may be represented holding a feeding bottle or the like." **(Illustration 40.)** "Tissue paper, which may have been previously cut out, pinked, pierced, edged, gathered or the like, is then wrapped or folded round the figure so as to

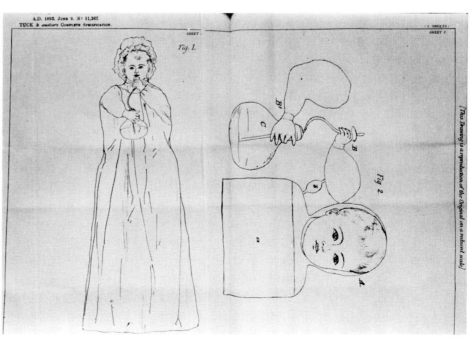

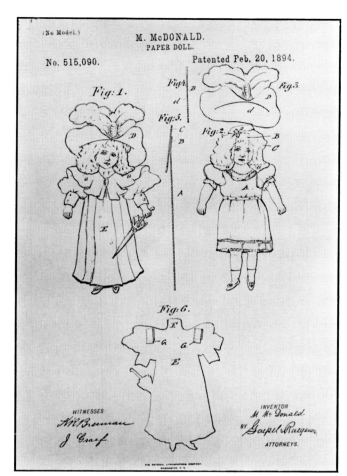

Illustration 41. A variation of the "The Heavenly Twins" using scrap pieces for the heads and hands. Father's head and shoulders measure 11in (28cm) high and the baby's head 3½in (9cm) high. Maurine Popp Collection.

RIGHT: Illustration 42. The February 20, 1894, United States Patent No. 515,090 issued to a Madge McDonald of Washington, District of Columbia, which was assigned to Raphael Tuck & Sons.

Illustration 43. British Patent No. 23,003 applied for by Adolph Tuck for the firm of Raphael Tuck & Sons, on November 30, 1893, and granted on October 6, 1894.

Illustration 44. *"Winsome Winnie" is No. 103 in the reduced size. She has her original tan envelope and three costumes. The doll and costumes are marked: "Artistic Series 103 and U.S. Patent Feb. 20th, 1894. Copyrighted by Raphael Tuck & Sons, Co., Ltd." The envelope measures 7in x 4¼in (18cm x 11cm) and the doll is 5½in (14cm) tall.*

resemble a baby's long robe or night dress, or the like, and a cap. To this treatment this material lends itself admirably, so that the figure becomes a capital representation of a baby dressed in the ordinary long robes of babyhood or the like." **Illustration 41** pictures a variation of The Heavenly Twins paper doll. No doubt the two heads and hands came from scrap pieces produced by the Tuck firm. The comical expression on the face of the father expresses the hope that the bottle he holds will silence the crying. The tissue paper clothing is constructed in a similar manner to the clothing of The Heavenly Twins.

As far as we can determine, Raphael Tuck & Sons applied for and was granted two British patents for paper dolls during the reign of Queen Victoria. Both of these patents, No. 11367 and No. 23003, list a Newnham Browne as the agent for the firm. **Color Illustration VII** shows a portion of a sheet of scrap pieces picturing the heads and arms that were used for "The Heavenly Twins."

On November 13, 1893, a United States Patent No. 515,090 was applied for by Madge McDonald of Washington, District of Columbia, and was granted to her on February 20, 1894. **(Illustration 42.)** We find that Madge McDonald evidently turned over the rights to this patent to the Tuck firm, allowing them to apply for the British Patent No. 23003 on November 30, 1893. **(Illustration 43.)** This patent was granted on October 6th, 1894, some eight months after the United States patent. These two patents were basically the same with the emphasis being put on the fact that the head was to be formed as a separate piece which could be pasted onto the top of an extension on the neck. This left the lower part of the face and hair free from and slightly in front of the neck and shoulders. The dress or costume was also constructed so that the neck of the dress could fit under the hair and chin. Both patents were listed as "Improvement in Printed Cardboard Dolls."

Madge McDonald's name appears on many of the paper doll box covers and envelopes published by Raphael Tuck & Sons. Along with the name, the patent date is listed as the one granted in the United States on February 20, 1894. Another

Illustration 45. *Shown is "Winsome Winnie" as No. 104 in the reduced size with her original tan envelope and three costumes. The doll and costumes are marked: "Artistic Series 104 and U.S. Patent Feb. 20th, 1894. Copyrighted by Raphael Tuck & Sons, Co., Ltd." Measurements are the same as Illustration 44.*

point of interest to be noted is that instead of Madge McDonald, she is also listed as Marguerite McDonald and even as Margaret McDonald.

The first series of paper dolls published by Raphael Tuck & Sons was "Our Pets Dressing Series." This series consists of three different sets, number one through number three. Each set is packed in a shallow cardboard box with the doll's name and her picture, dressed in one of her costumes, on the box. These three dolls from the "Our Pets Dressing Series" were published during Queen Victoria's reign at three different times and under three different markings. Number one was "Patent Applied For," number two was "Copyright Patent No. 23,003" and number three was "United States Patent February 20th, 1894." **Color Illustration VIII-A** shows the first of Tuck's paper dolls in this series, "My Lady Betty and Her Gowns," with her original box cover. **Color Illustration VIII-B** pictures the six colorful costumes and elegant flowery or feathered bonnets for her. At this point it is wise to remember that each of the three paper dolls from the "Our Pets Dressing Series," published under the British Patent No. 23,003 had six costumes instead of four that were used under the United States patent of February 20, 1894.

Set number two of this series is "Winsome Winnie and Her Wardrobe." **Color Illustration IX-A** shows her with her original box cover. **Color Illustration IX-B** shows the six colorful costumes and matching oversize bonnets for Winsome Winnie. These costumes lack the decoration found on the previously mentioned "My Lady Betty and Her Gowns." The third and final set in this series is "Dolly Delight and Her Dresses." In **Color Illustration X-A** she is pictured with her original box cover. **Color Illustration X-B** shows Dolly Delight's six rather plain, but colorful dresses and six large bonnets with feathered plumes.

Very little has been found of advertising for the paper dolls published by Raphael Tuck & Sons. However, **Color Illustration XI** pictures an extremely rare stand-up counter display advertisement. It is 20in (51cm) high and advertises "Patented Dressing Dolls" that have been described above. This particular doll features "Dolly Delight" dressed in one of her costumes.

A smaller size of the "Our Pets Dressing Series" was also published in tan-colored envelopes instead of the boxes used for the larger series. No doubt this was to make them available at a less expensive price. This series reduced the size of the dolls to 5½in (14cm). Each doll has three dresses and three hats. An interesting point that we would like to bring out once again is that each of the three dolls we have listed previously in the 10in (25cm) size had six dresses and six hats. Evidently, these costumes were divided and six sets were published under the American Patent No. 515,090 that was issued February 20, 1894. To clarify this, "My Lady Betty" became No. 101 and 102, "Winsome Winnie" became No. 103 and 104 and "Dolly Delight" became no. 105 and 106. The six original dresses from each set were split, making three costumes for each of these dolls. **Illustrations 44 & 45** show the method used.

Illustration 46 pictures a box in a light blue color with dark blue printing titled "Our Pets Dressing Series." The top edge of the box is marked: "One Doz. Sets, Our Pets, NO. 10." Apparently, there were 12 of the small enveloped sets originally in the box. One wonders if the small tan enveloped sets were also sold individually? Marked on the lower right side of each envelope were the words: "Copyright 1894, Raphael Tuck & Sons Comp' Ltd., New York, U.S. Patent February 20th, 1894." This marking brings up another question. Was this small size published only for the American market?

Illustration 47 shows the cover of a box featuring the three smaller size dolls and costumes from the "Our Pets Dressing Series." It is obvious from the box cover that this set was published for the French market. Our set is not complete but what we have makes it very interesting. We have Winsome Winnie and My Lady Betty. Dolly Delight is missing from our set. Each doll and each costume is marked on the back in French. For example: My Lady Betty and her costumes are marked with the Tuck easel and palette trademark, "Raphael Tuck & Fils Ltd. Editeurs Paris, Londres, New York. Par décret spécial Éditeurs de Sa Majesté lá Reine d'Anglettere. Déposé."

The second full-size series is the "Prince & Princess Dressing Series" consisting of four different sets, Artistic Series No. IV, V, VI and VII. In this series Tuck published both the American Patent No. 515,090 and the British Patent No. 23,003. The results are sometimes confusing. Many Tuck collectors do not realize that there are two sets of the Prince and Princess Series. The American sets have four dresses and four hats. The British sets have six costumes and six hats. The

Illustration 46. *A cover of a box that evidently held one dozen of the small size "Our Pets Dressing Series." It is marked with United States patent date of February 20, 1894. Size is 8¼in x 4½in (22cm x 12cm).*

Illustration 48-B. "Royal Regie" is shown with his four elaborate costumes. He is marked with the easel and palette trademark, "By Special Appointment, Publishers to Her Majesty the Queen, Raphael Tuck & Sons, London, Paris, New York, Artistic Series IV, U.S. Patent February 20th, 1894, copyright 1894 by Raphael Tuck & Sons Co., Ltd." The costumes are marked the same as the doll with the difference being in the number on each costume. Upper row, left to right, "Art Series IVC," "IVA," "IVB" and "IVD." The paper doll is 9¼in (24cm) tall. Herbert Hosmer Collection.

ABOVE: Illustration 47. This original box that contained the small size "Our Pets Dressing Series" is obviously a set made for the French market. The cover is marked: "Petite Mére et ses Petites Filles. Trois Poupées á Habiller avec leur Trousseau Complet. Raphael Tuck & Fils, Éditeurs, Paris. Librairie Artistique de la Jeuness." Size is 11in x 5½in (28cm x 14cm).

FAR LEFT: Illustration 48-A. The folder containing a "Royal Regie" paper doll and four costumes and hats. The cover carries the American patent date "Feb. 20th, 1894, Designed by Marguerite McDonald and Raphael Tuck & Sons, London, Paris, New York. Publishers to Her Majesty the Queen." The folder measures 10in x 6in (26cm x 15cm). Herbert Hosmer Collection.

ABOVE: Illustration 49-A. The folder containing a "Lordly Lionel" paper doll and four costumes. The cover carries the United States patent date "Feb. 20th, 1894. Designed by Marguerite McDonald and published by Raphael Tuck & Sons, London, Paris, New York. Publishers to Her Majesty the Queen." The folder measures 10in x 6in (26cm x 15cm).

LEFT: Illustration 49-B. "Lordly Lionel" is shown with his four elaborate costumes. He is marked with the easel and palette trademark, "By Special Appointment, Publishers to Her Majesty the Queen, Raphael Tuck & Sons, London, Paris, New York, Artistic Series V, U.S. Patent February 20th, 1894, copyright 1894 by Raphael Tuck & Sons Co., Ltd." The costumes are marked the same as the doll with the difference being in the number on each costume. Upper row, left to right, "Artistic Series VA" and "VB" and lower row, "VC" and "VD." The paper doll is 9¼in (24cm) tall.

ABOVE: Illustration 50-A. The original folder for "Sweet Abigail" and the doll herself. The folder reads "Sweet Abigail, Prince and Princess Series of Dressing Dolls, Patd. Feb. 20th, 1894. Designed by Marguerite McDonald. Raphael Tuck & Sons, London, Paris, New York. Publishers to Her Majesty the Queen." The doll is marked with the easel and palette trademark, "Publishers to Her Majesty the Queen, Raphael Tuck & Sons, London, Paris, New York, Artistic Series VI, U.S. Patent February 20th, 1894, copyright 1894 by Raphael Tuck & Sons Co., Ltd." The folder measures 10in x 6in (26cm x 15cm). The doll is 9¼in (24cm) tall.

RIGHT: Illustration 50-B. The four costumes for "Sweet Abigail" are shown here. They have the same marking as the doll with a different number on each costume. Reading from left to right, the first gown is marked: "Artistic Series VI A," the second is "Artistic Series VI B," the third "Artistic Series VI C" and the fourth "Artistic Series VI D."

names are changed but the dolls and the costumes are the same. The exception to this is that the American patented sets only have the four costumes as we have mentioned before.

"Royal Regie" was marked: "Artistic Series IV" and was published under the American Patent No. 515,090 that was dated February 20, 1894. **Illustration 48-A** shows the original folder for Royal Regie which is a flat folder-like package. This folder was published with either blue or pink lettering. Marguerite McDonald is listed as the designer and the folder is also marked: "Raphael Tuck & Sons, London, Paris, New York. Publishers to Her Majesty the Queen." **Illustration 48-B** pictures Royal Regie in his pink suit with darker pink polka dots, a gold chain and a white collar and cuffs. His costumes are marked: "Artistic Series IV-A," "IV-B," "IV-C" and "IV-D." Artistic Series IV-A is a gray costume with pink accessories and a pink cape. His hat is also gray with a pink plume. He holds a sword in his left hand. IV-B is a red costume with gray stripes. A red and dark gray cape is thrown over his shoulders and he has a dark gray hat with a large red plume and gold buckle. The IV-C costume is all gold with a large purple full-length cape and jeweled accessory around the shoulders. A gold crown with colored jewels is worn on his head. Artistic Series IV-D is an elaborate yellow costume with floral trim and a soft lavender-colored cape lined with fur. His crown is gold with colored jewels.

The same doll as Royal Regie was published under the British Patent No. 23,003 but was called "Prince Hyacinth." This set came in a flat box with a decorated cover. **(Color Illustration XII-A.)** Two additional costumes and hats came in this set that were not in the Royal Regie set. This made a total of six costumes and six hats for Prince Hyacinth. **Color Illustration XII-B** pictures Prince Hyacinth with his six costumes and hats. The costumes are marked: "Robe of State & Crown IV-A," "Court Ball Costume & Crown IV-B," "Morning Robe & Hat IV-C," "Visiting Robe & Hat IV-D," "Masquerade Costume & Hat IV-E" and the "Knight Templer Costume & Headpiece IV-F." Two of the costumes are designed for courtly appearance, three are fashioned for everyday use, while the sixth represents his knightly attire.

"Lordly Lionel" was marked: "Artistic Series V" and was published under the American Patent No. 515,090 on February 29, 1894. He has four costumes and four hats and is packaged within a flat folder. **Illustration 49-A** pictures the folder for Lordly Lionel. Marguerite McDonald is listed as the designer and the folder is also marked: "Raphael Tuck & Sons, London, Paris, New York. Publishers to Her Majesty the Queen." **Illustration 49-B** pictures Lordly Lionel in his white suit with blue sash and blue shoes. His costumes are marked: "Artistic Series V-A," "V-B," "V-C" and "V-D." Artistic Series V-A is a blue costume with a net and lace

Illustration 51-B. *The four costumes for "Courtly Beatrice" are shown here. They have the same marking as the doll, but with a different number on each costume. Reading from left to right, the first gown is marked: "Artistic Series VII A," the second is "Artistic Series VII B," the third "Artistic Series VII C" and the fourth "Artistic Series VII D."*

overblouse. He holds a bouquet of flowers in his right hand. His hat is blue with a white feather. Artistic Series V-B is a green and brown tunic-type costume trimmed with a feather. Artistic Series V-C is a lavender and white costume with a lavender cape. The large hat is lavender trimmed with a white plume. Artistic Series V-D is a green and gold costume with a gold-colored cape. He holds a falcon in his right hand. The matching hat has a large feather.

"Prince Darling" was published under the British Patent No. 23,003. This doll and four of his six costumes are the same as Lordly Lionel. **Color Illustration XIII-A** shows the flat box that came with Prince Darling, Prince Darling himself and his troubadour costume which is Artistic Series No. V-A. **Color Illustration XIII-B** pictures Artistic Series V-B Courtier Costume, Artistic Series V-C the Hunting Costume, Artistic Series V-D the Reception Costume, Artistic Series V-E the Hawking Costume and Artistic Series V-F the Leve Robe and Crown.

The third set in the "Prince & Princess Series" is titled "Sweet Abigail." **Illustration 50-A** pictures the original folder which contained the doll and her four costumes. Sweet Abigail is pictured with the folder. She is dressed in a white dotted swiss undergarment with a green sash. The band in her hair is green and her stockings and shoes are pink. **Illustration 50-B** pictures her four costumes and headpieces. The first gown is off-white with red ribbon decoration and a matching headpiece supporting a red feathered plume. This is marked: "Artistic Series VI-A." The second outfit is a courtly affair, a white gown with a lavender print. She wears a long purple lined gold, floor-length cape over her gown. The headpiece is a jeweled crown with a white plume. This outfit is marked: "Artistic Series VI-B." The third outfit is a deep pink party dress with a matching jeweled headband supporting a pink feather. Both pieces are marked: "Artistic Series VI-C." The fourth gown is blue with a small white pattern topped with a lace neck piece and it has a broad brim matching hat with a blue feather. These are marked: "Artistic Series VI-D." The paper doll issued under the British Patent No. 23,003 to match up with Sweet Abigail has not been found by us. We have to assume though that this set had the six costumes and six hats that would follow the other process used in the previous paper dolls from this series.

The last in the series of "Prince and Princess" is titled "Courtly Beatrice," Artistic Series VII. It was published under the United States Patent No. 515,090 which was issued on February 20, 1894. The original folder is pictured in **Illustration 51-A** and Courtly Beatrice herself stands alongside the folder wearing an underdress of white, laced up the front with blue ribbon. She has a blue ribbon in her hair and blue shoes and stockings. Courtly Beatrice has four costumes and four hats. The first costume is marked: "Artistic Series VII A." It is a dark green dress with a flowing light green robe. Her gold pocketbook and jeweled belt hang low from the waist. Her headpiece is missing. The second costume is marked: "Artistic Series VII B" and represents a court dress. It is red and white decorated with ropes of jewels and topped with a jeweled crown. The third costume is marked: "Artistic

ABOVE: Illustration 52. Pictured are three of the small size paper dolls from the "Prince and Princess Series of Dressing Dolls." "Lordly Lionel" is marked: "No. 108." "Sweet Abigail" is marked: "No. 109" and "Courtly Beatrice" is marked: "No. 110." These are shown in their tan-colored envelopes that contain a doll 5½in (14cm) tall with four costumes and four hats. Marked in the lower right corner of each envelope: "Copyright 1894 by Raphael Tuck & Sons Company Ltd."

Illustration 53-A. The cover of the original folder for the "Fairy Tale Series of Dressing Dolls". The paper doll is pictured with her "Red Riding Hood" costume. The folder is marked: "Patd. Feb. 20th, 1894 Raphael Tuck & Sons, London, Paris, New York. Publishers to Her Majesty the Queen." The folder measures 10in x 6in (26cm x 15cm).

45

BELOW: *Illustration 53-B.* Shown is the paper doll with her four costumes. The doll and her costumes have the same markings except for the addition of a letter after each costume. They are marked: "Raphael Tuck & Sons, London, Paris, New York Artistic Series VIII. Publishers to Her Majesty the Queen, United States Patent February 20, 1894. Copyright 1894 by Raphael Tuck & Sons Co., Ltd." Upper left represents "Little Miss Muffet VIII C," center is the doll VIII, upper right "Little Bo Peep VIII D," lower left "Mother Goose VIII B," and lower right "Little Red Riding Hood VIII A." Doll is 9in (23cm) tall.

BELOW RIGHT: *Illustration 54-A.* The original folder for "Cinderella of the Fairy Tale Series of Dressing Dolls." The folder reads "The Fairy Tale Series of Dressing Dolls, Patd. Feb. 20th, 1894. Raphael Tuck & Sons, London, Paris, New York. Publishers to Her Majesty the Queen." The doll is marked with the easel and palette trademark, "Publishers to Her Majesty the Queen, Raphael Tuck & Sons, London, Paris, New York. Artistic Series IX. United States Patent Feb. 20th, 1894. Copyright 1894 by Raphael Tuck & Sons Co., Ltd." The folder measures 10in x 6in (26cm x 15cm). The doll is 9¼in (24cm) tall.

Series VII C." This costume is green and white with puffy sleeves and a flaring oversized collar. The matching headpiece is trimmed with a large white plume feather. The fourth costume, Artistic Series VII D, is a blue walking costume with puffy sleeves and accented shoulders. A matching blue broad brim hat sports a large white feather. **(Illustration 51-B.)**

The same doll as "Courtly Beatrice" was published under the British Patent No. 23,003, but was called "Princess Mayblossom." This set comes in a flat box picturing the Princess and stating the following: "Princess Mayblossom & Her Court Costumes." In **Color Illustration XIV-A** this cover is shown with the doll standing next to the box cover. She is marked: "Princess Mayblossom Artistic Series No. VII." This set should have six gowns and six hats as we have shown in the previous British patented sets. Unfortunately, one costume and three hats are missing. **Color Illustration XIV-B** pictures the "Afternoon Gown" marked: "Artistic Series VII A." "The Fancy Gown" marked: "Artistic Series VIIB," "The Morning Gown" marked: "Artistic Series VIIC," "The Home Dress" marked: "Artistic Series VIID" and "The Garden Party Dress" marked: "Artistic Series VIIE."

Just as in the "Our Pets Dressing Series," we find that "The Prince and Princess Series of Dressing Dolls" was also published in a smaller size. These dolls were reduced in size to 5½in (14cm). These smaller sets contained four costumes and four hats. **(Illustration 52.)**

"The Fairy Tale Series of Dressing Dolls" is the next major grouping of paper doll sets published by Raphael Tuck & Sons. This series is made of three different sets, No. VIII, IX and X. These sets appear under the United States Patent No. 515,090 and the British Patent No. 23,003.

The white folder of set No. VIII pictures Little Red Riding Hood posed between two upright sprays of flowers attractively colored in red and gold. **(Illustration 53-A.)** This represents the United States issue of this set. **Illustration 53-B** pictures the doll with her costumes. The doll is in her white undergarments with a

LEFT: Illustration 54-B. *Costumes for the "Fairy Tale Dressing Series, Artistic Series No. IX."* The costumes are all marked: "Raphael Tuck & Sons, London, Paris, New York, Artistic Series IX. Publishers to Her Majesty the Queen, United States Patent February 20, 1894. Copyright 1894 by Raphael Tuck & sons Co., Ltd." The upper left is marked with the additional marking "Cinderella Artistic Series IXA," the one on the right is "The Fairy Godmother Artistic Series IXB," lower left is "Goody Two Shoes, Artistic Series IXC" and the lower right is "Cinderella at Home, Artistic Series IXD."

ABOVE: Illustration 55-A. *The original folder for the "Fairy Tale Series of Dressing Dolls."* It pictures a little boy in his "Little Boy Blue" costume posed between plants and with a bird house on top of the right hand group of flowers. This set is marked: "Artistic Series X. Patd Feb. 20th 1894. Raphael Tuck & Sons, London, Paris, New York. Publishers to Her Majesty the Queen." Folder measures 10in x 6in (26cm x 15cm). Herbert Hosmer Collection

RIGHT: Illustration 55-B. *The costumes and the doll for "Artistic Series No. X."* The doll and costumes all have the same markings except for the addition of a letter after each costume. They are marked: "Raphael Tuck & Sons London, Paris, New York, Artistic Series X. Publishers to Her Majesty the Queen. United States Patent February 20th 1894. Copyright 1894 by Raphael Tuck & Sons Co., Ltd." The costumes are left to right: "Prince Charming Artistic Series X A," "Dick Whittington, Artistic Series X B," the paper doll, "Artistic Series X," "Little Jack Horner, Artistic Series X C" and "Little Boy Blue, Artistic Series X D." Doll measures 9in (23cm). Herbert Hosmer Collection.

47

gold sash and bag hanging from her waist. She has a gold ribbon in her hair and wears short white socks and blue shoes. Artistic Series VIII A is "Little Red Riding Hood." This costume has a white pinafore over a blue dress and the usual red cape. She is carrying a basket of food in her left hand and a bouquet of flowers in her right hand. Her bonnet is also red. Artistic Series VIII B is "Mother Goose." This is a colorful black and red costume with a black cape lined in yellow. Her stockings are red and there are gold buckles on her shoes. She leads a white goose in front of her. Her black and red high peaked hat has a gold buckle. Artistic Series VIII C is "Little Miss Muffet." Her dress is a pale blue with an overdress of white dotted swiss. She wears short black lace gloves, carries a bowl in her right hand, a spoon in her left hand and a spider is seen at her left side. Her large hat is blue to match her dress and has a large blue feather on top. Artistic Series VIII D is "Little Bo Peep." Her dress is basically lavender and white with a white apron. Her stockings are lavender and her shoes purple. She carries a crook in her left hand. Her hat is straw with lavender trim.

The set marked: "Artistic Series No. VIII" that was issued under the British patent has not been available to us. This set would, of course, be the same as the above set with the additional number of costumes increased to six. The folder of set No. IX pictures a young girl dressed as Cinderella, posed between two upright floral sprays. On the right of the folder is the figure of a young girl. She is wearing a blue and white undergarment, has a gold ribbon in her hair and has blue shoes and stockings. **(Illustration 54-A.)** The first costume is "Cinderella at the Ball." It is an elaborately designed dress, basically white with a green and yellow design. The headpiece is dominated by three large white feathery plumes. She holds a white feather fan in her left hand. Both pieces are marked: "Artistic Series IX A." Her second costume is titled "The Fairy Godmother." The long flowing dress is white, flecked with tiny yellow stars; the long full-length cape is of the same material. A soft green and yellow sash circles her waist. Her wings are delicately colored in pale

BELOW: Illustration 56. An advertisement found on the backs of the paper doll boxes for the "Fairy Tale Dressing Series" that were issued under the British Patent No. 23,003. The size of the advertisement is 9⅞in x 6in (25cm x 15cm).

BELOW RIGHT: Illustration 57. This is found on the back of the boxes containing "The Belles of the Seasons" paper dolls and costumes. There were published under the British Patent No. 23,003. Size of the advertisement is 9⅞in x 6in (25cm x 15cm).

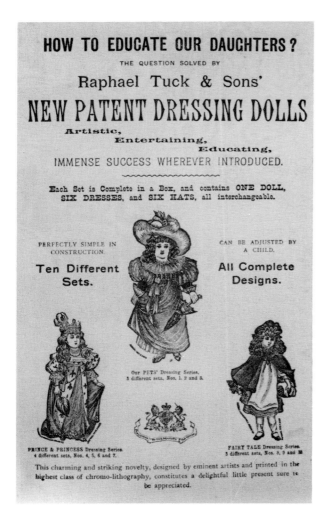

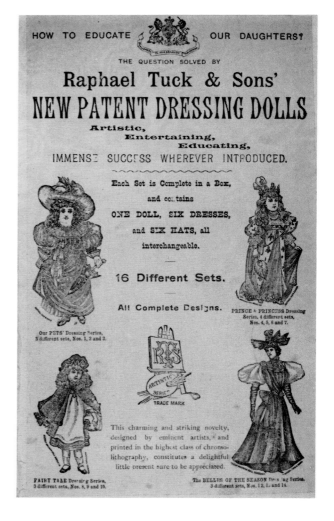

BELOW: Illustration 59. The "Belle of the West," Artistic Series XIII, Blonde and Brunette Series of Dressing Dolls is shown with her original box cover and four costumes. All dresses and the doll are marked as follows: the easel and palette trademark, "By Special Appointment, Publishers to Her Majesty the Queen, Raphael Tuck & Sons, London, Paris, New York. Artistic Series XIII. United States patent February 20th, 1894. Copyright 1894 by Raphael Tuck & Sons, Ltd." Box cover measures 9⁷⁄₈in x 6in (25cm x 15cm). The doll is 9in (23cm) tall.

ABOVE: Illustration 58. The "Belle of the South," Artistic Series XII, Blonde and Brunette Series of Dressing Dolls is shown with her original box cover and four costumes. All dresses and the doll are marked as follows: the easel and palette trademark, "By Special Appointment, Publishers to Her Majesty the Queen, Raphael Tuck & Sons, London, Paris, New York. Artistic Series XII. United States patent February 20th, 1894. Copyright 1894 by Raphael Tuck & Sons, Ltd." Box cover measures 9⁷⁄₈in x 6in (25cm x 15cm) The doll is 9in (23cm) tall. Maurine Popp Collection.

Illustration 60. *The "Belle of Newport," Artistic Series XIV, Blonde and Brunette Series of Dressing Dolls is shown with her original box cover and four costumes. All dresses and the doll are marked as follows: the easel and palette trademark, "By Special Appointment, Publishers to Her Majesty the Queen, Raphael Tuck & Sons, London, Paris, New York. Artistic Series XIV. United States patent February 20th, 1894. Copyright 1894 by Raphael Tuck & Sons, Ltd." Box cover measures 9⅞in x 6in (25cm x 15cm). The doll is 9in (23cm) tall. Maurine Popp Collection.*

Illustration 61. *The "Belle of Saratoga," Artistic Series XV, Blonde and Brunette Series of Dressing Dolls is shown with her original box cover and four costumes. All dresses and the doll are marked as follows: the easel and palette trademark, "By Special Appointment, Publishers to Her Majesty the Queen, Raphael Tuck & Sons, London, Paris, New York. Artistic Series XV. United States patent February 20th, 1894. Copyright 1894 by Raphael Tuck & Sons, Ltd." Box cover measures 9⅞in x 6in (25cm x 15cm). The doll is 9in (23cm) tall.*

Illustration 62. *The box cover of an early set of a paper dog and his various costumes, "Jolly Rover, Our Dog at School and Play." Marked: "New Series of Dressing Dolls, No. 35. Raphael Tuck & Sons Ltd., London, Paris and New York. Designed at the Studios in England. Printed in Saxony," also with the Tuck easel and palette trademark. Size of the box cover is 9½in high and 5¾in wide (24cm x 15cm). Maurine Popp Collection.*

yellow and pink. She wears a string of stars around her shoulder and a star-studded headpiece. She carries a long wand topped with a star in her left hand. The costume and headpiece are both marked: "Artistic Series IX B." The third costume is that of "Goody Two Shoes." It consists of a colorful peasant dress with a high laced waistline. She wears a wide brim floppy straw hat decorated with flowers. Both are marked: "Artistic Series IX C." The fourth costume is that of "Cinderella at Home." She is pictured in her work clothes and wearing a large white dust cap. She carries a broom in her hand. Both costume and hat are marked: "Artistic Series IX D." **(Illustration 54-B.)**

The British patented set of Artistic Series IX is contained in a flat box. The cover of the box reads: "The Fairy Tale Dressing Series No. IX." **Color Illustration XV-A** pictures the paper doll to the right of the box cover and is marked with the British Patent No. 23,003. Next to her is her very fancy costume titled "Cinderella at the Ball," Artistic Series IX A. **Color Illustration XV-B** pictures left to right, "The Fairy Godmother," Artistic Series IX B, "Goody Two Shoes," Artistic Series No. IX C, "Cinderella at Home," Artistic Series IX D and "Morgiana," Artistic Series IX E. The sixth costume representing Mother Hubbard is missing but her hat, Artistic Series IX F, is shown on the right.

The final set in "The Fairy Tale Series" is Artistic Series X. This is marked with the United States patent date of February 20, 1894. **Illustration 55-A** shows the original folder for this set that pictures a boy in his "Little Boy Blue" costume. **Illustration 55-B** pictures the four costumes and hats for him. "Prince Charming," Artistic Series X A, has a basic pink suit with royal purple inserts on the sleeves, waist and hips. His purple cape is lined in lavender. He carries a white slipper in his right hand. His purple headpiece is lavishly trimmed with jewels. The "Dick

Whittington" costume, Artistic Series X B, is a two-piece suit trimmed with a brown collar, belt, bag and brown boots. He carries a staff with a red kerchief tied to it and has his cat at his feet. A small close-fitting green cap serves as his headpiece. "Little Jack Horner," Artistic Series X C, has a basic purple suit with a white pinafore over it and a ruffled white collar. He holds a pie in his right hand. The headpiece is tan with a small grouping of flowers on the top. "Little Boy Blue," Artistic Series X D, wears a loose fitting blue smock and carries a horn in his right hand. His large hat is a darker shade of blue with a feather the color of the smock.

The British version of Artistic Series X was published under Patent No. 23,003. **Color Illustration XVI-A** pictures the paper doll in his two-piece blue suit with the original box cover to his left and his "Prince Charming" (Artistic Series X A) costume to his right. **Color Illustration XVI-B** pictures "Little Boy Blue," Artistic Series No. X D, "Dick Whittington," Artistic Series X B, "Jack the Giant Killer," Artistic Series No. X E, in the center, "Jack and the Bean Stalk," Artistic Series X F and "Little Jack Horner," Artistic Series X C. As usual, the British patent features six costumes instead of the four costumes in the United States patent.

As we have mentioned before, very little has been found in the way of advertising for Tuck paper dolls. **Illustration 56** shows an advertisement for "Our Pets Dressing Series," "Prince and Princess Dressing Series" and the "Fairy Tale Dressing Series." These three series were issued under the British Patent No. 23,003. The ad appears on the back of the boxes containing the "Fairy Tale Dressing Series" only. The two other series have an ad on the back of each box advertising a competitive venture conducted by Adolph Tuck. (See **Illustration 13** in Part I).

After publishing many beautiful, colorful paper dolls representing children, the Tuck firm decided to publish several series of paper dolls with adult figures. Judging from the elaborate costumes for these dolls, one has to reflect on the idea that perhaps they hoped to attract an entirely different group of people, namely the adult world.

The patent drawings for the British Patent No. 23,003 and the United States Patent No. 515,090 showed children as the featured figures. Even though the above mentioned adult figure paper dolls were an entirely different design from the children, the same patent numbers were used for these sets. This indicates the fact that it was not the actual drawing pictured in the patent paper that was important, but the conception of what could be accomplished by using this idea. Quote: "The figure to be represented is cut (stamped) out of thick paper, cardboard or the like and printed preferably in colours, to represent the intended figure. It is convenient

Illustration 63. The cover of a wonderful paper soldier set, "Who Would Not Be a Soldier Brave." This is from the "New Series of Dressing Dolls" and is numbered No. 37. It is marked: "Raphael Tuck & Sons, Ltd., London, Paris, New York." The box measures 13½in x 12in (34cm x 31cm). Jean Woodcock Collection.

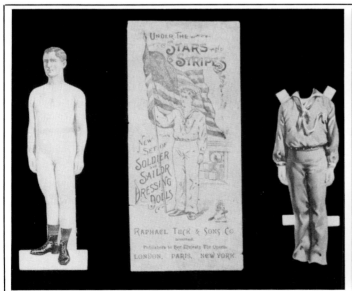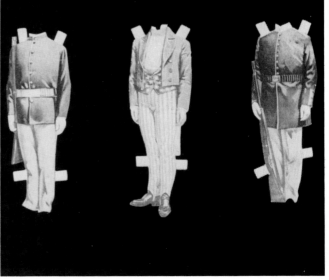

Illustration 64. An unusual set of an adult figure with his costumes titled "Under the Stars and Stripes." "New Set of Soldier and Sailor Dressing Dolls." Marked with the easel and palette trademark, "Raphael Tuck & Sons. Co. Limited. Publishers to Her Majesty the Queen, London, Paris, New York." Only the envelope has these markings. The figure and costumes have no marking at all. Paper doll is 7¼in (18cm) tall. Original envelope is 8½in (22cm) x 3¾in (22cm x 10cm). Maurine Popp Collection.

Illustration 65. *The original box for the set for the small size "Dear Dorothy" paper doll. This particular set was obviously published for the French market. Size of box cover: 9½in x 6in (24cm x 15cm). Maurine Popp Collection.*

Illustration 66. *The small size "Dear Dorothy" of the "Dolls For All Seasons" series. Her original envelope and four costumes are pictured with her. The Artistic Series numbers found on the larger size doll do not appear on this size. Doll and costumes are marked with the easel and palette trademark, "By Special Appointment. Publishers to Her Majesty the Queen. Raphael Tuck & Sons Ltd., London, Paris, New York. Designed at the Studio in New York and printed at the Fine Art Works in Bavaria." Envelope size 9½in x 6in (24cm x 15cm). Doll size 9in (22cm).*

that the head should be formed of a separate piece which may be stuck on to the top of an upward extension of the neck, thus having say the lower part of the face and hair free from and slightly in front of the neck and shoulders." One of the principal points of these two patents seems to be this method of applying the head to the neck, allowing the dresses to slip under the chin and hair.

After the "Fairy Tale Series of Dressing Dolls," Raphael Tuck & Sons published "The Belles of the Season Dressing Dolls." There are three different sets which are titled "Lady Margaret and Her Gowns," "Lady Clare and Her Costumes" and "Lady Lilian and Her Gowns." An advertisement for these sets is found on the back of the boxes containing these paper dolls. **(Illustration 57.)** "The Belles of the Season Series" was published under the British Patent No. 23,003. Each boxed set contains a paper doll with six costumes and six hats. The first doll in this series is marked: "Lady Margaret Artistic Series XII." **Color Illustration XVII-A** pictures the cover of the box and Lady Margaret herself. **Color Illustration XVII-B** pictures her six costumes. They are as follows: Artistic Series XII A, "Bridal Gown;" Artistic Series XII B, the "Ball Dress;" Artistic Series XII C, the "Dinner Dress;" Artistic Series XII D, her "Morning Costume;" Artistic Series XII E, her "Afternoon Gown" and Artistic Series XII F is called a "Reception Gown."

"Lady Clare and Her Costumes" is the second set in this Artistic Series group. **Color Illustration XVIII-A** pictures Lady Clare with her original box cover. She is marked: "Lady Clare Artistic Series XIII." **Color Illustration XVIII-B** pictures her costumes as follows: Artistic Series XIII A, "Country Walking Costume;" Artistic Series XIII B, "Garden Party Costume;" Artistic Series XIII C is missing; Artistic Series XIII D is her "Afternoon Costume;" Artistic Series XIII E is missing; Artistic Series XIII F is "The At Home Dress."

The third set of the "Belles of the Season Series" is "Lady Lilian and Her Gowns." **Color Illustration XVIV-A** pictures Lady Lilian with the cover of her original box. She is marked: "Lady Lilian, Artistic Series XIV." Her costumes are pictured in **Color Illustration XVIV-B**. They are as follows: Artistic Series XIV A, "Visiting Costume;" Artistic Series XIV B, "Afternoon Gown;" Artistic Series XIV C, "Dinner Dress;" Artistic Series XIV D, "Lawn Tennis Costume;" Artistic Series XIV E, "In the Park" and Artistic Series XIV F, "At the Ball." The back covers of the boxes of the "Belles of the Season Dressing Dolls" all carry the advertisement shown in **Illustration 57**. This ad features the "Our Pets Dressing Series," "The Prince & Princess Dressing Series," "The Fairy Tale Dressing Series" and finally, the "Belles of the Season Dressing Series."

Under the United States Patent No. 515,090 that was granted on February 20, 1894, the Tuck firm published a series of adult ladies called, "Blonde and Brunette Series of Dressing Dolls." These were "Belle of the South," Artistic Series XII; "Belle of the West," Artistic Series XIII; "Belle of Newport," Artistic Series XIV and "Belle of Saratoga," Artistic Series XV.

All the gowns and dolls for this series were marked with the easel and palette trademark, "By Special Appointment" Publishers to Her Majesty the Queen. Raphael Tuck & Sons, London, Paris, New York. U.S. Patent February 20th, 1894 Copyright 1894 by Raphael Tuck & Sons, Ltd." **Illustration 58** pictures "Belle of the South," Artistic Series XII. Reading from left to right from the top row we see XII A. The gown and long gloves are red with white puffed sleeves and a red and white bow and sash on the right side. The hat has a red bow with a white feather. XII doll has dark brown hair, wears a white chemise and petticoat trimmed with pink eyelet. She has a pink ribbon around her neck. XII B is a blue two-piece walking suit with light tan stand-up collar and trim on the hem. The buttons and gloves are also light tan. A matching blue hat with tan-colored feather completes the outfit. XII C is a two-piece dress with the tunic and skirt a soft green with red

BELOW: Illustration 67. The small size "Rosey Ruth" of the "Dolls For All Seasons" series. She is pictured with her four costumes and hats. The Artistic Series numbers found on the larger size doll do not appear on this size. Doll and costumes are marked with the easel and palette trademark, "By Special Appointment. Publishers to Her Majesty the Queen. Raphael Tuck & Sons Ltd., London, Paris, New York. Designed at the Studio in New York and printed at the Fine Art Works in Bavaria." Doll size 9in (22cm).

BELOW RIGHT: Illustration 68. The small size "Merry Marion" of the "Dolls For All Seasons" series. She is pictured with her four costumes and hats. The Artistic Series numbers found on the larger size doll do not appear on this size. Doll and costumes are marked with the easel and palette trademark, "By Special Appointment. Publishers to Her Majesty the Queen. Raphael Tuck & Sons Ltd., London, Paris, New York. Designed at the Studio in New York and printed at the Fine Art Works in Bavaria." Doll Size 9in (22cm).

and brown stripes. She has a white blouse with large pale yellow cape sleeves and trim around the shoulders. Her gloves are white. The skirt hem also has a pale yellow band. Her hat is pale yellow with red and green bows. The original folder is shown in the bottom center. It reads: "Belle of the South, Blonde and Brunette Series of Dressing Dolls. Pat. Feb. 20th, 1894. Raphael Tuck & Sons London, Paris, New York. Publishers to Her Majesty the Queen. Designed by Marguerite McDonald." XII D is a white dress with red trim around the neck and ruffles bound in red. A rope-like band is shown for her hair with a white feather.

Illustration 59 pictures "Belle of the West," Artistic Series XIII. Reading from left to right from the top row we see XIII A. An afternoon dress is two-pieced with red stripe trim. The underblouse and neck band are red and her gloves are light tan. A natural color straw hat is shown with a red ribbon trim. XIII doll has light brown hair and wears a white chemise and petticoat trimmed with yellow ribbon and a yellow bow at her waist. A black ribbon band is around her neck with a gold jewel. XIII B is a green evening gown with black lace trim. A white rope-like trim is around the neckline and hem of the dress. The gloves are white and she has a green ribbon and bow around her neck. The hat is white with green trim. XIII C is a pink evening gown trimmed with black ribbon. The cape is ermine and she has long tan gloves and carries a white feather fan. The hat is white and pink feathers. The original folder is shown in the bottom center. It reads: "Belle of the West, Blonde and Brunette Series of Dressing Dolls. Patd. Feb. 20th, 1894. Raphael Tuck & Sons. London, Paris, New York. Publishers to her Majesty the Queen. Designed by Marguerite McDonald." XIII D is a formal gown, lavender in color with purple ribbon trim, accented by a white and lavender stripe cape over sleeve, sash and large bows. A purple rope-like band is shown for her hair with a green feather.

Illustration 70-B. *"The Bridal Party Series of Dressing Dolls."* *Four costumes for the bride. From top to bottom: Ball Gown, Artistic Series 600 B; Walking Costume, Artistic Series 600 C: Golfing Costume, Artistic Series 600 D; Bridal Gown, Artistic Series 600 A.*

Illustration 60 pictures "Belle of Newport," Artistic Series XIV. Reading from left to right from the top row we see XIV A. A pale blue evening gown with eyelet trim, gold bow at the waist and shoulder. A gold necklace with blue jewels matches the dress. The doll XIV has blonde hair, a white chemise and petticoat trimmed with lavender ribbon and she wears a jeweled necklace which matches the ribbon on the chemise. XIV B is an amber-colored gown with black lace trim on the bodice and the skirt. She has matching long gloves and red flowers fastened at the neckline. XIV C is a formal white gown with dark red puffy sleeves and a tiny floral pattern trimming the skirt, waist and neckline. Her long white gloves are stitched in red and she is carrying a matching red feather fan. The necklace is gold with red jewels. The original folder is shown in the bottom center. It reads: "Belle of Newport." Blonde and Brunette Series of Dressing Dolls. Patd. Feb. 20th, 1894. Raphael Tuck & Sons, London, Paris, New York. Publishers to Her Majesty the Queen. Designed by Marguerite McDonald." XIV D is a two-piece tennis dress, white with blue dots. The over sleeves and sleeves below the elbow are dark blue. She has brown gauntlet-style gloves and carries a tennis racquet.

Illustration 61 pictures "Belle of Saratoga," Artistic Series XV. Reading from left to right from the top row we see XV A. A ball dress in pale lavender with purple trim. The ribbon and bow at her neck are purple and she carries a bouquet of purple violets. Her long gloves are white. The doll XV has light brown hair and wears a white chemise and petticoat trimmed with blue ribbon. A gold necklace with pale blue jewels complements her gown. XV B is a two-piece walking suit of pale gray with a red bow, buttons and trim at the hemline. Her gloves are a light tan color. Her hat is mulberry-colored with a gray feather. XV C is a lovely white bridal gown trimmed with orange blossoms. Her gloves are white. The original folder is shown in the lower center. It reads: "Belle of Saratoga, Blonde and Brunette Series of Dressing Dolls. Patd. Feb. 20th, 1894. Raphael Tuck & Sons, London, Paris, New York. Publishers to Her Majesty the Queen. Designed by Marguerite McDonald."

Some of the dolls and some of their costumes that we see in the "Belles of the Season" series and the "Belles Series" are identical. This can cause a great deal of confusion. We have compiled a chart showing the problems that can be encountered.

Illustration 70-A. *"The Bridal Party Series of Dressing Dolls."* *The bride is shown with her original box cover and she is Artistic Series 600. They are marked with the easel and palette trademark, By Special Appointment. Publishers to Her Majesty the Queen. Raphael Tuck & Sons, London, Paris, New-York. U.S. patent February 20th, 1894 by Raphael Tuck & Sons Co. Ltd, New-York." Doll size 9½in (24cm). Box size 10in x 6in (25cm x 15cm).*

Illustration 71-A. *"The Bridal Party Series of Dressing Dolls." The bridegroom is Artistic Series 601 and he is shown with his original box cover. The markings are the same as for the bride. Doll size 9½in (24cm). Box size 10in x 6in (25cm x 15cm).*

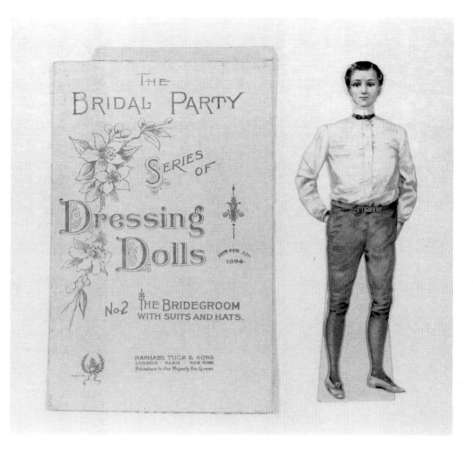

Illustration 71-B. *"The Bridal Party Series of Dressing Dolls." four costumes for the bridegroom. Reading from left to right: Wedding suit, Artistic Series 601 A; Outdoor suit, Artistic Series 601 B; Uniform, Artistic Series 601 C; Lounge jacket and pants, Artistic Series 601 D.*

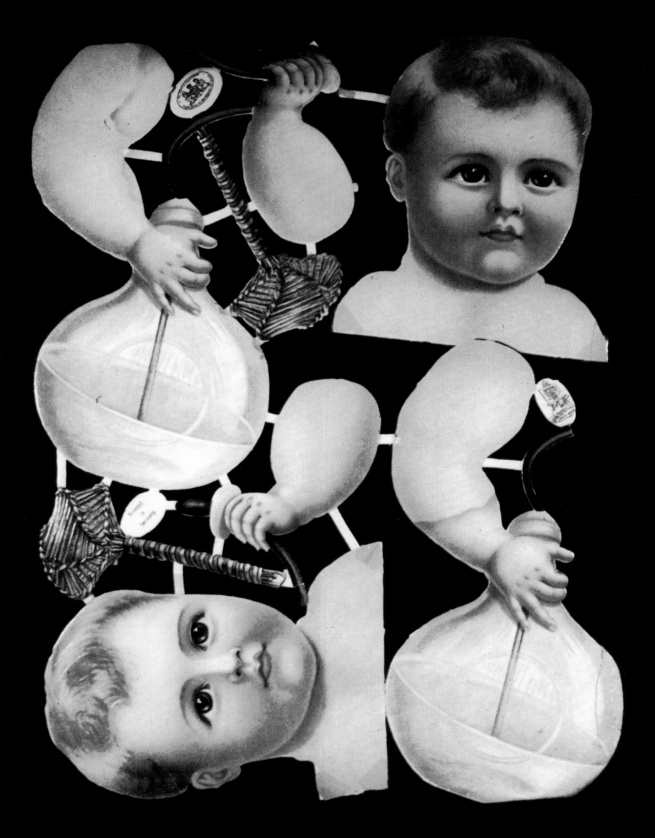

Color Illustration VII. *A portion of a sheet of colorful scrap material used to construct ornaments. When completed with the addition of a tissue skirt, each figure measures 32¼in (82cm) long.*

LEFT: Color Illustration VIII-A. *The original box cover is marked: "My Lady Betty and Her Gowns, Our Pets Dressing Series No. 1, Patent Applied for, Raphael Tuck & Sons, London, Paris and New York, Publishers to Her Majesty the Queen." The doll is marked with the Tuck easel and palette mark, also, "By Special Appointment, Publishers to Her Majesty the Queen, Copyright Patent Applied For, Raphael Tuck & Sons, London, Paris, New York, Designed at the Studios in England and Printed at the Fine Art Works in Bavaria, Artistic Series I." The box cover measures 10½in high by 6in wide. (26cm x 5cm).*

Color Illustration VIII-B. *"My Lady Betty, Artistic Series I." The clothing has the same markings as the doll in Color Illustration VIII-A, but starting from the top left to right the costumes are marked: "Artistic Series IA," "IB," "IC," "ID," "IE" and "IF." The doll stands 10in (26cm) tall.*

LEFT: Color Illustration IX-A. Shown is the original box cover and the doll "Winsome Winnie." The markings are the same as "My Lady Betty" with one exception. "Winsome Winnie" is marked: "Artistic Series II." The size of the box cover and the doll are the same as "My Lady Betty."

Color Illustration IX-B. Pictured are the costumes for "Winsome Winnie." They have the same markings as "My Lady Betty" but starting from the left top, they are marked: "Artistic Series IIA," "IIB," "IIC," "IID," "IIE" and "IIF."

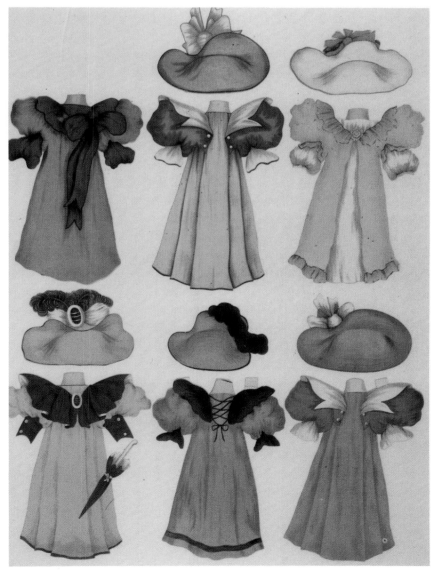

LEFT: Color Illustration X-A. Shown is the original box cover and the doll "Dolly Delight." The markings are the same as "My Lady Betty" and "Winsome Winnie" with one exception. She is marked: "Artistic Series III." The size of the box cover and the doll is the same as "My Lady Betty" and "Winsome Winnie."

Color Illustration X-B. Pictures are the costumes for "Dolly Delight". They have the same markings as "My Lady Betty" and "Winsome Winnie" but starting from the left top, they are marked: "Artistic Series IIIA, IIIB, IIIC, IIID, IIIE and IIIF."

Color Illustration XI. *A stand-up counter display advertisement for "Tuck's Patented Dressing Dolls." She represents "Dolly Delight" in one of her costumes. Size is 20in (51cm) tall.*

Color Illustration XII-B. "Prince Hyacinth & His Fancy Dress Costumes, No. IV." This pictures the Prince and six costumes, each with a hat. The figure and each costume is marked with the easel and palette trademark. They are also marked: "Raphael Tuck & Sons, London, Paris, New York, Publishers to Her Majesty the Queen, Designed at the Studios in England and Printed at the Fine Art Works in Bavaria, Copyright, Patent No. 23,003, Artistic Series IV." The doll stands 9in (23cm) tall. Peggy Jo Rosamond Collection.

Color Illustration XII-A. The flat box in which "Prince Hyacinth" was packaged. The title reads: "Prince Hyacinth & His Fancy Dress Costumes, Prince & Princess Dressing Series No. IV., Raphael Tuck & Sons, London, Paris, New York, Publishers to Her Majesty the Queen, Patent No. 23,003." Box measures 10 x 6in (26cm x 15cm). Peggy Jo Rosamond Collection.

ABOVE: Color Illustration XIII-A. *"Prince Darling With his Troubadour Costume No. VA." He is shown standing next to the original box. The title reads: "Prince Darling, The Prince & Princess Dressing Series No. V, Raphael Tuck & Sons, London, Paris, New York, Publishers to Her Majesty the Queen, Patent No. 23,003." Box measures 10in x 6in (26cm x 15cm). The paper doll is 9in (23cm) tall. Peggy Jo Rosamond Collection.*

Color Illustration XIII-B. *"Prince Darling" and each of his costumes are marked with the easel and palette trademark, also "Raphael Tuck & Sons, London, Paris, New York, Publishers to Her Majesty the Queen, Designed at the Studios in England and Printed at the Fine Art Works in Bavaria." They are also marked: "Copyright, Patent No. 23,003, Artistic Series V." Peggy Jo Rosamond Collection.*

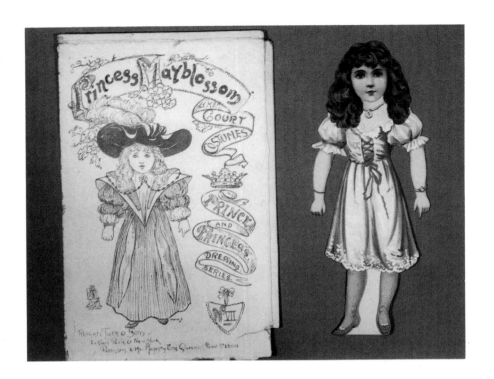

LEFT: Color Illustration XIV-A. The original cover is shown with the Princess standing next to it. It states the following: "Prince and Princess Dressing Series Princess Mayblossom & Her Court Costumes, No. VII, Raphael Tuck & Sons, London, Paris, New York, Publishers to Her Majesty the Queen, Patent No. 23,003." The doll is marked: "Princess Mayblossom Artistic Series No. VII". She is 9¼in (24cm) tall and the cover is 10in x 6in (26cm x 15cm).

Color Illustration XIV-B. Pictured are "Princess Mayblossom's" gowns. Upper left is the "Afternoon Gown" marked: "Artistic Series No. VII-A," upper right is the "Fancy Gown" marked: "Artistic Series No. VII-B," center is the "Morning Gown" marked: "Artistic Series No. VII-C," lower left is "The Home Dress" marked: "Artistic Series No. VII-D" and lower right is the "Garden Party Dress" marked: "Artistic Series VII-E." Dress No. VII-F is missing.

Color Illustration XV-A. The original box cover is shown with the paper doll and one of her costumes. The box is marked: "Cinderella At Home, Goody Two Shoes, The Fairy Godmother, Cinderella at the Ball, Morgiana, Mother Hubbard, No. IX, Raphael Tuck & Sons, London, Paris, New York, Publishers to Her Majesty the Queen, Patent No. 23,003" and the easel and palette trademark. The doll has the additional marking: "By Special Appointment" and the costume has the same marking plus the name "Cinderella at the Ball." The box cover measures 10in x 6in (26cm x 15cm). The doll stands 9¼in tall (24cm).

Color Illustration XV-B. All four costumes are for "The Fairy Tale Dressing Series No. IX." The four costumes pictured are marked as follows; "The Fairy Godmother IX-B," "Goody Two Shoes IX-C," "Cinderella at Home IX-D," "Morgiana IX-E" and the hat for "Mother Hubbard IX-F, British Patent No. 23,003."

Color Illustration XVI-A. Pictured is the original box cover that is marked: "The Fairy Tale Dressing Series No. X." Its contents are; "Prince Charming," "Dick Whittington," "Boy Blue," "Jack Horner," "Jack the Giant Killer," "Jack and the Bean Stalk" and "Raphael Tuck & Sons, London, Paris, New York, Publishers to Her Majesty the Queen, Patent No. 23,003," also the easel and palette trademark. The doll has the additional marking: "By Special Appointment" and the costume has the same marking plus the name "Prince Charming." The box measures 10in x 6in (26cm x 15cm) while the doll stands 9in (24cm) tall.

Color Illustration XVI-B. Pictured are five costumes for the British version of "Artistic Series X" published under the British Patent No. 23,003. Top left is "Little Boy Blue, Artistic Series XD," center is "Jack the Giant Killer, Artistic Series XE," top right is "Dick Whittington, Artistic Series XB," lower left is "Jack and the Bean Stalk, Artistic Series XF" and lower right "Little Jack Horner, Artistic Series XC."

LEFT: Color Illustration XVII-A. *"Lady Margaret and Her Gowns" is the title on the original box cover containing a paper doll and six costumes. This is from the "Belles of the Season, Series No. XII." The box cover is marked with the easel and palette trademark and "Raphael Tuck & Sons, London, Paris, New York, Publishers to Her Majesty the Queen, Patent No. 23,003." The doll has the same markings found on the box cover except for her name "Lady Margaret." Box cover measures 9⅞in x 6in (25cm x 15cm) and the doll is 9in (23cm) tall.*

BELOW: Color Illustration XVII-B. *"Lady Margaret" and her six gowns. Pictured left to right on the top row is "The Bridal Costume, Artistic Series XII-A," "The Ball Dress, Artistic Series XII-B" and the "Dinner Dress, Artistic Series XII-C." On the lower row, from left to right we have "A Morning Costume, Artistic Series XII-D," an "Afternoon Gown, Artistic Series XII-E" and a "Reception Dress, Artistic Series XII-F." The doll and all costumes are marked with the easel and palette mark and "By Special Appointment, Publishers to Her Majesty the Queen, Raphael Tuck & Sons, Ltd., London, Paris, New York, Designed at the Studios in England and Printed at the Fine Art Works in Bavaria." Also, all are marked: "Copyright, Patent No. 23,003, Artistic Series XII."*

Color Illustration XVIII-A. *"The Lady Clare and Her Costumes" is the title of the second box set in the "Belles of the Season Series." It carries No. XIII. The box cover is marked with the easel and palette trademark and "Raphael Tuck & Sons, London, Paris, New York, Publishers to Her Majesty the Queen, Patent No. 23,003." "Lady Clare" has the same markings as those found on the box cover except that her name, "Lady Clare," appears on the back of the doll. The box cover measures 9⅞in x 6in (25cm x 15cm). The doll is 9in (23cm) tall.*

Color Illustration XVIII-B. *The second set in this series of "The Belles of the Season Dressing Dolls" is "Lady Clare and Her Costumes." Two of her gowns are missing. Left to right we see "Country Walking Costume, Artistic Series XIII-A," "Garden Party Costume, Artistic Series XIII-B," "Artistic Series XIII-C" is missing, "Afternoon Costume, Artistic Series XIII-D," "Artistic Series XIII-E" is missing and "The At Home Dress, Artistic Series XIII-F." The costumes are marked with the easel and palette trademark and "By Special Appointment, Publishers to Her Majesty the Queen, Raphael Tuck & Sons Ltd., London, Paris, New York, Designed at the Studios in England and Printed at the Fine Art Works in Bavaria." Also, all are marked: "Copyright Patent No. 23,003, Artistic Series XIII."*

Color Illustration XIX-A. *"Lady Lilian and Her Gowns" is the title of the third set in "The Belles of the Season Series, No. XIV." The cover is marked with the easel and palette mark and "Raphael Tuck & Sons Ltd., London, Paris, New York, Publishers to Her Majesty the Queen, Patent No. 23,003." "Lady Lilian" has the same markings as those on the cover. The box measures 9-⅞in x 6in (25cm x 15cm). The paper doll is 9in (23cm) tall. Lady Lilian's gowns are pictured in* Color Illustration XIX-B *on page 89.*

Illustration 72-B. *"The Bridal Party Series of Dressing Dolls." Four costumes for the maid of honor who is Artistic Series No. 602. From top to bottom: Wedding Party Dress, Artistic Series 602 B; Afternoon Gown, Artistic Series 602 A; Formal Afternoon Gown, Artistic Series 602 D; Afternoon Gown, Artistic Series 602 C.*

Illustration 72-A. *"The Bridal Party Series of Dressing Dolls." Artistic Series No. 602. The maid of honor with the cover of her original box. The markings are the same as the bride. Doll size 9½in (24cm). Box size 10in x 6in (25cm x 15cm).*

Illustration 73-A. *"The Bridal Party Series of Dressing Dolls." Artistic Series No. 603. The bridesmaid with the cover of her original box. The markings are the same as the bride. Doll size: 9½in (24cm). Box size: 10in x 6in (25cm x 15cm).*

Gowns and Dolls that are Identical

Belle of Saratoga XV		Lady Margaret XII
XV C	XIIA	
XV A	XIIF	
XV B	XIID	
Belle of the South XII		Lady Clare
XII C	XIIIB	
XII B	XIIID	
XII D	XIIIF	
Belle of Saratoga XV		Lady Clare
XV D	XIIIA	
Belle of the South XII		Lady Margaret XII
XII A	XIIE	
Belle of the West XIII		Lady Lilian XIV
XIII B	XIVA	
Belle of the West XIII		Lady Margaret XII
XIII D	XIIC	
Belle of the West XIII		Lady Lilian XIV
XIII B	XIVA	
Belle of Newport XIV		Lady Margaret XII
XIV A	XIIB	
Belle of Newport XIV		Lady Lilian XIV
XIV B	XIVB	
XIV D	XIVD	
XIV C	XIVC	

Identical Dolls

Belle of the South XII	Lady Margaret XII
Belle of Saratoga XV	Lady Lilian XIV
Belle of the West XIII	Lady Clare XIII

From the "New Series of Dressing Dolls" we find "Jolly Rover" with a sub-title "Our Dog at School and Play." **Illustration 62** shows the original box cover for this set. He stands upright by means of an easel pasted on his back and is dressed in a school outfit with his school bag and slate. Included in his wardrobe is a military outfit, an evening robe, four headdresses and four pairs of slip-on shoes. It appears that one outfit is missing. Take notice of the various dog pets included with the costumes. **(Color Illustration XX.)**

If we have a dog paper doll, it figures that there should also be a cat. Unfortunately, the box cover is missing but we believe this set also is a part of the "New

Illustration 73-B. "The Bridal Party Series of Dressing Dolls." Four costumes for the bridesmaid who is Artistic Series No. 603. Reading from left to right: Bridesmaid Gown, Artistic Series 603 A; Two-Piece Walking Costume, Artistic Series 603 B; Rowing Costume, Artistic Series No. 603 C; Bicycle Outfit, Artistic Series 603 D.

Illustration 74. *"Favorite Faces" Novel Series of Dressing Dolls. Miss Ada Rehan. The figure is marked with the easel and palette trademark, "Raphael Tuck & Sons Ltd., London, Paris, New-York. Publishers to Her Majesty the Queen. Miss Ada Rehan A. U.S. Patent February 20th, 1894." Her four costumes are all marked in the same manner with some additions. Reading from left to right: Miss Ada Rehan as "Katherine" in* Taming of the Shrew IA. *Miss Ada Rehan as "Olivia" in* Twelfth Night IIA. *Miss Ada Rehan as "Lady Teazle" in* School for Scandal IIIA. *Miss Ada Rehan as "Mistress Ford" in* Merry Wives of Windsor IVA. *Doll is 9½in (24cm).*

Illustration 75. *"Favorite Faces" Novel Series of Dressing Dolls. Miss Julia Marlowe. The figure and her costumes are marked with the same markings as Miss Ada Rehan with some additions. Instead of "A," Miss Julia Marlowe is marked: "B." Reading from left to right: Miss Julia Marlowe as "Barbara Frietchie" IB. Miss Julia Marlowe as "Colinette" IIB. Miss Julia Marlowe as "Constance in* Love Chase IIIB. *Miss Julia Marlowe as "Rosalind" in* As You Like It IVB. *Doll is 9½in (24cm).*

Series of Dressing Dolls." She is dressed in a peasant costume and holds a doll in her right paw. Her first costume is blue with a white collar and apron. She carries a school bag and a book under her arm marked: "Musik." A bag of candy is under her left arm. The second costume is basically green with a white apron and bodice. She is carrying two kittens; one is dressed in a sailor suit holding a bottle of milk and the other is in an infant sacque. A third kitten stands at her side dressed in a pink dress and wide-brimmed pink hat. The third costume has a blue skirt with a shawl over the shoulders. She holds a cup and saucer marked: "Zum Geburtst." A small cat stands at her side. The costumes come with bonnets and slip-on shoes. **(Color Illustration XXI.)**

Illustration 63 pictures the box cover for a paper soldier from the "New Series of Dressing Dolls." It is titled "Who Would Not Be a Soldier Brave?" **Color Illustration XXII** pictures the soldier on horseback with six military uniforms and accessories. It is possible that the six matching pieces of headgear are missing.

Another set that possibly could be from the "New Series of Dressing Dolls" is pictured in **Color Illustration XXIII**. The doll is standing in front of a fence. Her three costumes are particularly beautiful. Her pale blue dress has a white pinafore that holds three doves. One dove is perched on her right hand. A small basket of flowers is at her feet. The second dress is a soft lavender. She holds a white kitten in her arms and a basket holding three other kittens is at her feet. The third costume is a red coat trimmed with white fur. A white dog is at her feet. Each costume has a matching hat and slip-on shoes.

"Our Little Treasure, From School Days to Womanhood" is another in the "New Series of Dressing Dolls," No. 39. **Color Illustration XXIV-A** pictures the doll, her original box cover and her lovely bridal gown. **Color Illustration XXIV-B** pictures the remaining five costumes, the school dress, afternoon dress, evening dress, and finally the traditional mourning dress.

Very few men paper dolls are found in Raphael Tuck & Sons publishing efforts. Contained in a light brown envelope we find a set titled "Under the Stars and Stripes," "New Set of Soldier and Sailor Dressing Dolls." The gentleman has three military costumes and one representing Uncle Sam. **(Illustration 64.)**

During this period of the reign of Queen Victoria, it has become clear that Raphael Tuck & Sons really became exceptionally successful in the publishing of paper dolls and their costumes. More and more series were added with a great deal

Illustration 76. "Favorite Faces" Novel Series of Dressing Dolls. Mrs. Leslie Carter. The figure and her costumes are marked with the same markings as Miss Ada Rehan with some changes. Instead of being marked "A," Mrs. Leslie Carter is marked "C." Reading from left to right: Mrs. Leslie Carter as "The Heart of Maryland" IC. Mrs. Leslie Carter as "ZaZa" Act III, IIC. Mrs. Leslie Carter as "Zaza" Act II, IIIC. Mrs. Leslie Carter as "Zaza" Act V, IVC. Doll is 9½in (24cm).

of imagination. The firm seemed to be successful in predicting what the young people of the time wanted and needed. Color played a major part in this and it was produced with great expertise. Perfection seemed to be a very important part of anything Raphael Tuck & Sons published.

A series called "Dolls For All Seasons" was published featuring four different dolls and their costumes. This series included "Dear Dorothy," Artistic Series 500; "Rosey Ruth," Artistic Series 501; "Merry Marion," Artistic Series 502 and "Sweet Alice," Artistic Series 503. This series was published in two sizes, a 13in (33cm) doll and a 9in (23cm) doll. The 13in (33cm) doll has the head formed as a separate piece which could be pasted onto the top of an extension on the neck. This left the lower part of the face and hair free from and slightly in front of the neck and shoulders, allowing the costumes to be slipped up under the hair and chin. (United States Patent No. 515,090.) The 9in (23cm) doll is printed in one piece with slits in the shoulder line cut through the long hair for the costume tabs. The 13in (33cm) doll is marked with the Artistic Series numbers but these numbers do not appear on the smaller size.

Color Illustration XXV-A pictures the original box cover to "Dolls For All Seasons, Dear Dorothy," Artistic Series 500, with two of her brightly colored costumes. **Color Illustration XXV-B** pictures "Dear Dorothy" with her other two costumes, bringing the total of costumes for her to four. **Illustration 65** shows an original box cover for the small 9in (23cm) size of "Dear Dorothy." This particular set was definitely published for the French market. It reads: "Mes Poupées à Deux charmantes Poupées á habiller avec leur trousseau. Raphael Tuck & Fils Ltd. Editeurs. Paris, Londres, Berlin, New-York." The 9in (23cm) dolls of the "Dolls For All Seasons" were each published with four costumes and four hats. The dolls and their wardrobes were each contained in a light brown envelope constructed of a thin inexpensive paper. **Illustration 66** pictures "Dear Dorothy," Artistic Series 500 with her original envelope. **Illustration 67** pictures "Rosey Ruth," Artistic Series 501. **Illustration 68** is "Merry Marion," Artistic Series 502 and the last in this series is pictured in **Illustration 69**. She is "Sweet Alice," Artistic Series 503.

Illustration 77-A. Miss Maude Adams from the "Favorite Faces" Novel Series of Dressing Dolls. She is marked: "Miss Maude Adams D." The box cover is marked: "Pat. Feb. 20th, 1894. Raphael Tuck & Sons. London, Paris, New York. Publishers to Her Majesty the Queen." Doll is 9½in (24cm). Box cover is 10in x 6in (26cm x 15cm).

Illustration 77-B. The costumes for Miss Maude Adams, reading from left to right, are as follows: Miss Maude Adams as "Dorothy" in Christopher Jr, ID. Miss Maude Adams as "Juliet" in Romeo and Juliet, IID. Miss Maude Adams as "Lady Babbie" in The Little Minister, IIID. Miss Maude Adams as the "Gypsy" in The Little Minister, IVD.

Illustration 78-A. *The original box cover for "Darling Hilda" reads as follows: "Darling Hilda and Her Wardrobe, New Series of Dressing Dolls. Designed by Marguerite McDonald. Patd. Feb. 20th 1894. Raphael Tuck & Sons London, Paris, New York. Publishers to Her Majesty the Queen." Box cover measures 10in x 6in (26cm x 15cm).*

Over the years, a subject that always seems to draw favorable attention has been the subject of weddings. Whether it is theater, opera, fashion, toys or paper dolls, using weddings as a theme seems to be inevitably successful. With its always very "up date" publishing efforts, Raphael Tuck & Sons published a most successful and beautiful series called "The Bridal Party Series of Dressing Dolls." This series featured "The Bride," Artistic Series 600; "The Bridegroom," Artistic Series 601; "The Maid of Honor," Artistic Series 602 and "The Bridesmaid," Artistic Series 603. Each figure has four costumes and is packaged in a shallow box container. They all have the same markings — the easel and palette trademark, "The Bridal Series of Dressing Dolls. By Special Appointment. Publishers to Her Majesty the Queen. Raphael Tuck & Sons, London, Paris, New-York. U.S. Patent February 20th, 1894 by Raphael Tuck & Sons Co. Ltd. New-York." **Illustration 70-A** pictures the original box cover and the bride. She is Artistic Series No. 600 and is dressed in pink and white undergarments. **Illustration 70-B** features her four costumes. Artistic Series 600 A is the bridal gown, a lovely soft green and white combination with a large white bow at her left shoulder. Artistic Series 600 B is an elegant ball gown in a soft creamy color and she has a long pink boa around her neck. Artistic Series 600 C shows a gown with a blue and white stripe blouse and skirt and an overskirt and bolero of blue with light brown trim. Artistic Series 600 D is the bride's golfing costume. It has a bright red jacket and a green and brown plaid skirt. The bridegroom is shown in **Illustration 71-A** with the original box cover and he is

Illustration 79. *The original box cover, the paper doll and the costumes for "Darling Edith and Her Wardrobe," New Series of Dressing Dolls. She is marked: "By Special Appointment. Publishers to Her Majesty the Queen. Raphael Tuck and Sons. London, Paris New York. Artistic Series No. 22. U.S. Patent February 20th 1894. Copyright 1894 by Raphael Tuck and Sons Co. Ltd." Each costume is marked the same as "Darling Edith" with one exception. She is Artistic Series No. 22 instead of No. 21. The coat next to the doll is Artistic Series No. 22 A. Lower left is Artistic Series No. 22 B, Artistic Series 22 C and Artistic Series No. 22 D. Box measures 10in x 6in (26cm x 15cm). Doll measures 9in (23cm).*

Illustration 80. *"Darling Muriel and Her Wardrobe," New Series of Dressing dolls. She is Artistic Series No. 23. She is marked in the same manner as "Darling Edith" but her costumes are marked, reading from left to right: "Artistic Series No. 23 A," "Artistic Series 23 B," "Artistic Series 23 C" and "Artistic Series No. 23 D." Doll measures 9in (23cm).*

wearing a white shirt, blue tie and blue pants. He is Artistic Series No. 601. **Illustration 71-B** features his four costumes. Artistic Series 601 A is his wedding attire, a formal black suit with tails and a white shirt and vest. Artistic Series 601 B shows blue and tan stripe pants with a light brown sports jacket and vest. Artistic Series 601 C is a blue U.S. military uniform. Artistic Series No. 601 D is his lounging outfit, a brown jacket and light gray checked pants. **Illustration 72-A** pictures the original box cover and the maid of honor. She is Artistic Series No. 682 and is dressed in white undergarments lavishly trimmed with blue ribbon. **Illustration 72-B** pictures her four costumes. Artistic Series 602 A is her afternoon gown, white with small blue dots and wide blue ribbon trim. Artistic Series 602 B is the maid of honor gown in soft lavender with lavish creamy-colored ribbon trim. The bow on her left shoulder matches the bow on the bridal gown. Artistic Series 602 C is an afternoon dress with a pink and green patterned blouse and skirt insert. The skirt is dark green. Artistic Series 602 D is a more formal afternoon gown of a soft pale pink lavishly trimmed with ribbon. **Illustration 73-A** pictures the original box cover and the bridesmaid. She is Artistic Series 603. Her undergarments are white trimmed with ruffles and pink ribbon. **Illustration 73-B** pictures her four costumes. Artistic Series 603 A is her bridesmaid gown in a soft blue trimmed with darker blue wide ribbon. Artistic Series 603 B is her two-piece walking costume, light brown jacket, plaid skirt and dark brown boa. Artistic Series 603 C is her rowing costume. The skirt and sleeveless jacket are blue trimmed in red and the blouse is white with red dots. Artistic Series 603 D is a bicycle outfit, soft gray and red plaid skirt with a red and white stripe blouse.

The Tuck publishing firm must have found that the adult paper doll figures were successful. They continued to publish these sets for some time. As we have mentioned before, there was "The Belles of the Season" series, published under the British Patent No. 23,003. This series included Lady Margaret, Lady Clare and Lady Lilian. The next adult figures represented dolls from the "Belles" series, published under the United States Patent No. 515,090. They are Belle of the South, Belle of the West, Belle of Newport and Belle of Saratoga. Following this series we have the Bridal Set, Artistic Series No. 600, The Bride, Bridegroom, Maid of Honor and the Bridesmaid. The final series of adult figures during Queen Victoria's reign appears to be "Favorite Faces Novel Series of Dressing Dolls, a series of English actresses. This series is marked in a different manner from those we have mentioned before. They are marked: "A,B,C,D." **Illustration 74** pictures Miss Ada Rehan. She is marked with the easel and palette trademark and "Raphael Tuck & Sons, Ltd., London, Paris, New-York. Publishers to Her Majesty the Queen. Miss Ada Rehan A. U.S. patent February 20th, 1894." Her four costumes are marked in the same way. Each costume represents a personality she played on the stage. Reading from left to right: Miss Ada Rehan as "Katherine" in *Taming of the Shrew*, IA. A basic red gown with overdress of light brown trimmed in green. Miss Ada Rehan as "Olivia" in *Twelfth Night* IIA. A lavender tunic dress with lavender cape trimmed in gold and lavender stockings. Miss Ada Rehan as "Lady Teazle" in *School for Scandal*, IIIA. A two-piece gown with a red bodice trimmed with lace. The long sleeves are a pale blue brocade. The skirt is red, also lace-trimmed with an overskirt and bustle of blue brocade to match the sleeves. Finally, Miss Ada Rehan as "Mistress Ford" in *Merry Wives of Windsor* IVA. An extremely elaborate evening gown with lace underskirt, sleeve and collar trim. The bodice is pale gold with an overskirt and bustle of the same color.

Illustration 75 pictures the second set of "Favorite Faces," Novel Series of Dressing Dolls, Miss Julia Marlowe. The doll and her costumes are marked in the same way as Miss Ada Rehan except that Julia Marlowe is marked B instead of A. Each of the four costumes represent a personality she played on the stage. Reading from left to right: Miss Julia Marlowe as "Barbara Frietchie," IB. The gown is white with a printed green floral design. It is lavishly trimmed with pink ribbon and roses. Her shawl is white with pink trim. Miss Julia Marlowe as "Colinette," IIB. This coat is bright red trimmed with gray fur. She carries a gray fur muff. Miss Julia Marlowe as "Constance" in *Love Chase*, IIIB. This appears to be a two-piece riding costume. The skirt and trim on the bodice sleeves are a deep red and the bodice is green with a wide white collar. She holds a riding crop in her gloved hand. Miss Julia Marlowe as "Rosalind" in *As You Like It*, IVB. Her leggings and top appear to be brown leather and she wears a cape lined with a dark green fabric.

Illustration 76 pictures the third set of "Favorite Faces," Novel Series of Dressing Dolls, Mrs. Leslie Carter. The doll and her costumes are marked in the

Illustration 81-A. Above is the original box cover for "Gentle Amy" of the "Little Sunbeams" series. Gentle Amy herself is shown above the box cover. She is marked: "Artistic Series No. 701." Box cover measures 10in x 6in (26cm x 15cm). Doll measures 9½in (24cm). Maurine Popp Collection.

same way as Miss Ada Rehan, except that Mrs. Leslie Carter is marked C instead of A. Each of the four costumes represents a personality she played on the stage. Reading from left to right: Mrs. Leslie Carter as "The Heart of Maryland," IC. This is a lovely two-piece white gown, lavishly trimmed in blue. She has a white lace-trimmed bertha over the bodice. She also holds a blue and white striped shawl over her arm. Mrs. Leslie Carter as "Zaza" Act III, IIC. This features a two-piece gown with a bolero-style jacket. The skirt is black with swirls of red trim. Her jacket is light brown with red lapels and a high neck collar in black. Mrs. Leslie Carter as "Zaza" Act II, IIIC. Her blouse is white with a green lining and a high neck black collar. The skirt is bright red with a wide flounce on the bottom. Mrs. Leslie Carter as "Zaza" Act V, IVC. A beautiful white gown with abundant lace trim. Her cape is a soft orange color with a pale green lining. The large bow on her shoulder matches the lining of the cape. **Illustration 77-A** pictures the original box cover and Miss Maude Adams from the "Favorite Faces" Novel Series of Dressing Dolls. The box cover reads as follows: "Favorite Faces, Novel Series of Dressing Dolls," the easel and palette trademark, "Pat. Feb. 20th 1894 No. 2. Miss Maude Adams, Raphael Tuck & Sons, London, Paris, New York. Publishers to Her Majesty the Queen." The number 2 shown on the box does not appear anywhere else. The paper doll is marked in the same manner as Miss Ada Rehan except that Miss Maude Adams is marked "D" instead of "A" as Miss Ada Rehan is. The doll is wearing very elaborate undergarments. A lavender corset, trimmed in white and a white petticoat with five rows of ruffles is seen. She wears lavender and white striped stockings. **Illustration 77-B** pictures the four costumes for Miss Maude Adams. They are marked, reading from left to right: Miss Maude Adams as "Dorothy" in *Christopher Jr.*, ID. This costume is a sheer white with an underskirt of pale green. The skirt has strips of white ruching with yellow flowers. Miss Maude Adams as "Juliet" in *Romeo and Juliet*, IID. This is a lovely white lace gown with a lining in soft blue. Beadwork appears around the shoulder and lower part of the bodice. Miss Maude Adams as "Lady Babbie" in *The Little Minister*, IIID. An elegant evening gown of white brocade has a soft yellow floral design. The square collar and center panel of the skirt is fine lace. She holds a dark brown shawl at her back. Miss Maude Adams as the "Gypsy" in *The Little Minister*, IVD. Her skirt is a dark gray lined in red and she has a red plaid shawl tied around her hips. Her blouse is white with a red collar and belt. She also wears a double strand of blue beads.

Illustration 81-B. Four costumes for "Gentle Amy" of the "Little Sunbeams New Series of Dressing Dolls." Reading from left to right they are: Artistic Series No. 701 A, Artistic Series No. 701 B, Artistic Series 701 C and Artistic Series No. 701 D. Maurine Popp Collection.

Illustration 82. *"Charming Helen" of the "Little Sunbeams New Series of Dressing Dolls" with her four costumes. She is marked: "Artistic Series No. 702" and her costumes are marked as follows: reading left to right, "Artistic Series No. 702 A," "Artistic Series No. 702 B," "Artistic Series 702 C" and "Artistic Series No. 702 D." Doll measures 9¼in (24cm). Joyce Alexander Collection.*

Illustration 83. *"Pretty Maude" of the "Little Sunbeams New Series of Dressing Dolls" with her four costumes. She is marked: "Artistic Series No. 703" and her costumes are marked, reading from left to right: "Artistic Series No. 703 A," "Artistic Series No. 703 B," "Artistic Series No. 703 C" and "Artistic Series No. D." Doll measures 9¼in (24cm). Jan Banneck Collection.*

"Darling Hilda," Artistic Series No. 21, "Darling Edith," Artistic Series No. 22 and "Darling Muriel," Artistic Series No. 23 are all from the "New Series of Dressing Dolls." **Illustration 78-A** pictures the cover of the box for "Darling Hilda." It is also marked: "New Series of Dressing Dolls. Patd. Feb. 20th, 1894. Raphael Tuck & Sons, London, Paris, New York," the easel and palette trademark, "Publishers to Her Majesty the Queen. Designed by Marguerite McDonald." **Illustration 78-B** pictures "Darling Hilda" with her four costumes. She is marked: "Artistic Series 21." She has long blonde hair with a blue ribbon around her head. Her chemise is blue and white and her stockings and shoes are black. Her costumes are as follows: Artistic Series 21 A is a white dress with yellow and green print. The bouffant sleeves are yellow with green trim and the full gathered cape top is yellow, green and white. Artistic Series 21 B is a soft blue trimmed in white. A white sash and bow is draped across the front of the dress. Artistic Series 21 C is a pale lavender coat with purple ribbon trim. Artistic Series 21 D is a red dress trimmed with white lace and ribbon. Matching hats are shown for each costume. "Darling Edith and Her Wardrobe" is Artistic Series 22. She is pictured in **Illustration 79** with her original box cover and her four dresses and hats. The cover is marked in the same way as "Darling Hilda." "Darling Edith" is wearing a soft green chemise with white polka dots and white lace trim. Her stockings are black with pale green embroidery and her shoes are also black. Her dresses are as follows: Artistic Series 22 A is an elegant blue, ankle-length coat with darker blue braid trim and white buttons. Artistic Series 22 B is also a coat, in soft pink with green trim. Artistic Series 22 C is a dark green dress with an underblouse of soft yellow and finally,

Illustration 84-A. The original envelope for "Little Martha. The Colonial Belles. Her Hats and Her Gowns." It is marked: "Raphael Tuck & Sons Co. Ltd. London, Paris, New-York. Publishers to Her Majesty the Queen. No. 750." Envelope measures 9½in x 6in (24cm x 15cm).

Illustration 84-B. "Little Martha" with her four costumes. Reading from left to right, we have "Artistic Series No. 750 A," "Artistic Series No. 750 B," "Artistic Series No. 750" (the paper doll) and "Artistic Series D." Doll measures 9in (23cm).

Artistic Series 22 D is a red dress with white dots and a large white lace collar with lace trim on the bottom of the skirt. **Illustration 80** pictures "Darling Muriel," Artistic Series No. 23 of the New Series of Dressing Dolls. She is wearing a blue chemise, buttoned down the side, with white lace and ribbon trim. Her stockings and shoes are blue. The costumes for "Darling Muriel" are different from those of Artistic Series 21 and 22. They are knee length compared to the ankle length found in the costumes of the other dolls. Artistic Series 23 A is a dark lavender dress with purple trim. Her side-button leggings are tan and her shoes lavender. Artistic Series 23 B is a red coat with a white design. The three-tiered cape has two rows of white eyelet trim and one tier the same color as the coat. The side-button leggings are tan. Artistic Series 23 C is another coat in pink with a three-tiered cape in white. It also has the tan side-button leggings. Artistic Series 23 D has a white skirt and a green and yellow three-quarter coat, buttoned on the side. The side-button leggings are gray. Matching hats are shown for each outfit.

The "Little Sunbeams" series of Dressing Dolls was published with four different sets. Artistic Series No. 700, Artistic Series No. 701, Artistic Series No. 702 and Artistic Series No. 703. Artistic Series No. 700 is not pictured. **Illustration 81-A** pictures "Gentle Amy" with her original box cover. She has dark brown hair drawn into a knot on the top of her head. Her undergarments are white with a green corset tied at the waist in a pink bow. Her stockings are brown and her shoes black with pink bows. She is marked: "By Special Appointment. Publishers to Her Majesty the Queen. Raphael Tuck & Sons, London, Paris, New York. Artistic Series No. 701. U.S. Patent, February 20th, 1894 by Raphael Tuck & Sons, Co. Ltd. New York." Her box cover reads as follows: "Little Sunbeams, New Series of Dressing

Illustration 85-A. The original envelope for "Little Janice. The Colonial Belles. Her Hats and Her Gowns." It is marked: "Raphael Tuck & Sons Co., Ltd. London, Paris, New-York. Publishers to Her Majesty the Queen. No. 751." Envelope measures 9½in x 6in (24cm x 15cm).

Illustration 85-B. "Little Janice" with her four costumes. Reading from left to right, we have "Artistic Series No. 751 A." "Artistic Series No. 751 B," "Artistic Series No. 751" (the paper doll)," "Artistic Series No. 751 C" and "Artistic Series No. 751 D." Doll measures 9in (23cm).

ABOVE: *Illustration 86-B. The center spread of the* Dolly's Dressmaker *book. It shows two paper dolls and their costumes. Doll measures 5in (13cm).*

RIGHT: *Illustration 86-A. The cover for the* Dolly's Dressmaker *book. It is marked: "Copyright 1896, Raphael Tuck & Sons Ltd. London, Paris, New York. Publishers to the Queen." Book measures 7in x 10in (18cm x 25cm).*

Dolls, No. 2 (Artistic Series 701) Gentle Amy. Raphael Tuck & Sons London, Paris, New York. Publishers to Her Majesty the Queen. Pat' Feb. 20th 1894" and the easel and palette trademark. **Illustration 81-B** pictures her four costumes and three hats. We would like to state here that on the back cover of each original box of the Little Sunbeam Series a paper label has been placed stating that each of the "Little Sunbeams" sets has four dresses but only THREE hats. This series differs from other sets that almost every time have had four dresses and four hats to match the dresses. "Gentle Amy's" dresses are marked in the same manner as she is except for the addition of a letter after No. 701. Pictured left to right: Artistic Series 701 A is a brown and tan striped dress with a white pinafore. She has a pink cradle at her feet with her doll dressed in blue. Artistic Series 701 B in a pink party dress with a white yoke. Her stockings are pink and her shoes brown with pink bows. Artistic Series 701 C is a purple coat trimmed with gray fur and she carries a gray fur muff. Her leggings are light brown. Artistic Series 701 D is a red cape trimmed with ermine over a green striped skirt. A large green bow is tied at the neck and she has an ermine muff to match the cape. Her leggings are light brown. Her two hats and ribbon headpiece match the outfits.

 Illustration 82 pictures "Charming Helen" with her four dresses and three hats. She is marked in the same way as "Gentle Amy" except that she is Artistic Series No. 702. "Charming Helen" has dark brown hair. Her undergarments are very colorful. The bodice is a soft pink trimmed with white and the skirt is pale yellow. Her stockings are black. Reading from left to right we see a pretty dark red coat with gold buttons. This is worn over a green and white striped skirt. Her leggings are light brown. This is marked: "Artistic Series 702 A." Next to her coat is a white dress with purple ribbon trim, a purple belt and large purple bow on the shoulder. This dress is marked: "Artistic Series 702 B." To the right of the doll is a two-piece outfit. The blouse is pale pink with a darker pink print and the skirt is a light brown with wide bands of dark brown and red trim. This outfit is marked: "Artistic Series No. 702 C." The dress on the far right is a white sailor-style outfit. The trimming bands and the tie are a dark blue. This is Artistic Series No. 702 D.

 Illustration 83 pictures "Pretty Maude" with her four dresses and hats. She is marked in the same way as "Gentle Amy" except that she is Artistic Series No. 703. "Pretty Maude" has shoulder-length blonde hair and wears white undergar-

BELOW LEFT: Illustration 87-A. The cover of the book, Dolly's Dresses Painting Book. Judging by the costumes, this figures to be approximately 1896-1901. Book size is 8in x 10½in (20cm x 27cm).

BELOW: Illustration 87-B. A page from the book, Dolly's Dresses Painting Book. Page measures 8in x 10½in (20 x 27cm).

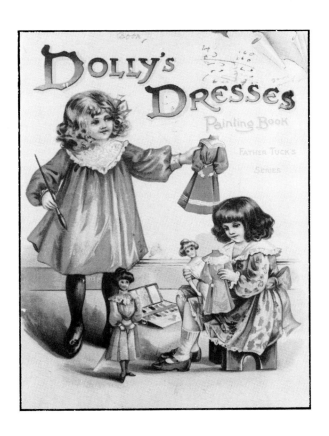

Baby Beatrice waiting to be Dressed.

Margery's Mother has made her some new Clothes.

ments with a blue corset and a pink sash. Her stockings are blue and she wears brown shoes. Reading from left to right we see pictured a white gown with a pale lavender print that is trimmed with dark purple ribbon. She has dark brown laced-up boots. This is Artistic Series No. 703 A. Next to this dress is a yellow gown over a pink and white stripe skirt and bodice. She has rose-colored beads and a fan attached to the beads and wears rose-colored stockings. The hat pictured with her is not original to this dress but is appropriate. This is Artistic Series 703 B. To the right of this dress is a green jacket with a green and white skirt. She is pushing a carriage that shows a doll dressed in red. This is Artistic Series No. 703 C. The last costume pictured is a red coat with green buttons. It has green and white stripes on the shoulder, a white skirt and a gray fur scarf and muff. Her leggings are red.

"The Colonial Belles Series" appears to have only two different dolls. "Little Martha" is Artistic Series No. 750 and "Little Janice," No. 751. However, the same dolls and their clothing also were published previously under the reign of Queen Victoria, but under different numbers and markings. Maurine Popp has this early set marked as follows: "Little Martha" marked: "Publishers by Royal Warrant, Artistic Series No. 36" and "Little Janice" marked: "Publishers by Royal Warrant, Artistic Series No. 35."

The Tuck company published many items such as these with the same dolls but different numbers causing some confusion for collectors. This should help to clear up the confusion for collectors who have the same dolls with the different numbers shown above. "Little Martha" from the Colonial Belles Series was published in a thin light tan envelope with brown lettering. It read: "Little Martha, The Colonial Belles. Her Hats and Her Gowns." She is pictured on the envelope.

Additional markings appear as follows: The Raphael Tuck easel and palette trademark, "No. 750. Raphael Tuck & Sons Co. Ltd. London, Paris, New-York. Publishers to Her Majesty the Queen." **(Illustration 84-A.) Illustration 84-B** pictures "Little Martha" and her gowns. They are marked with the easel and palette trademark, "By Special Appointment. Publishers to Her Majesty the Queen. Raphael Tuck & Sons Ltd. London, Paris, New York." The doll is marked: "Artistic Series No. 750." She has white hair with lavender ribbon around her head. Her chemise is white and she has dark purple stockings and brown shoes with pink bows. Reading from left to right we see Artistic Series 750 A. This is a colorful two-piece gown. Her blouse is white and the skirt and laced bodice are orange. The sleeves are gathered with black ribbon and a black bow is on her left side. Artistic Series 750 B has a yellow skirt and underblouse with a purple bodice and overskirt. Artistic Series 750 C has a pink and rose stripe skirt with a white trimming at the hem. The bodice has a colorful print with green leaves that match the green overskirt. Artistic Series 750 D is the same design as Artistic Series A using a blue and white print with darker blue ribbon trim. These gowns are all very similar in design but with the use of a variety of colors, they give the appearance of being different. **Illustration 85-A** pictures the envelope for "Little Janice," the second doll in this series. The markings are the same as those for "Little Martha" with the exception of the name "Little Janice" and "No. 751." **Illustration 85-B** pictures "Little Janice" and her four costumes. These are very similar in design to Little Martha's gowns and variety has been achieved by use of many bright colors. Her costumes are marked, reading from left to right: "Artistic Series No. 751 A," "Artistic Series No. 751 B," "Artistic Series No. 751 C" and "Artistic Series No. 751 D."

Illustration 87-D. A page from the book, Dolly's Dresses Painting Book. *Page measures 8in x 10½in (20cm x 27cm).*

Ethel wants some fresh Frocks.

Dolly's Dressmaker is a combination paper doll and doll pattern book. It was published in 1896 by Raphael Tuck & Sons. Information inside the book reads as follows: "This book will show you how to make new dresses for your dear Dolly, so you will have something to do on a rainy day and Dolly will always look lovely." The book contains three paper dolls with their costumes in color. Following each paper doll are patterns to fit a 9in (23cm) doll. **Illustration 86-A** pictures the cover of the *Dolly Dressmaker* book and **Illustration 86-B** pictures two of the paper dolls in the book. The doll on the left is blonde with white underclothes trimmed in blue. Her coat and hat are brown, trimmed with fur. Her blue blouse and skirt are trimmed in white and her pinafore is a soft pink color. Accessories such as hats, gloves, shoes and toys are also pictured. The doll on the right is a brunette in white underclothes. Her pinafore is white with pink ribbon trim, her short double-breasted jacket is brown, her dress is blue trimmed with pink and white lace and her coat is tan with a blue lining to match her dress. She also has accessories such as hats, gloves, shoes and toys.

Dolly's Dresses Painting Book is a charming book marked: "Father Tuck's Series Published by Raphael Tuck & Sons Co., Ltd. Designed at the Studios in England and New York, London, Paris. No. 2542." The book contains eight sheets of paper dolls with their clothes and accessories in full color. Each sheet has a duplicate in

Illustration 88. *"Dolly Darling" with her trunk and costumes. She is marked: "Artistic Series No. 1." Her costumes are marked: "Artistic Series 1 A," "Artistic Series 1 B" and "Artistic Series 1 C." Trunk measures 7¼in x 5in (19cm x 13cm). Doll measures 6½in (17cm). Maurine Popp Collection.*

86

Illustration 89. "Dolly Daisy" with her trunk and costumes. She is marked: "Artistic Series No. 3." Her costumes are marked: "Artistic Series 3 A," "Artistic Series 3 B" and "Artistic Series 3 C." Trunk measures 7¼in x 5in (19cm x 13cm). Doll measures 6½in (17cm).

black and white for painting. The back cover shows a doll with one dress and one hat. When the paper dolls and their clothes are cut, there are no markings. The following is a listing of the page titles:

1. Baby Beatrice waiting to be Dressed.
2. Ethel wants some fresh Frocks.
3. Margery's Mother has made her some new Clothes.
4. Connie and her walking Costumes.
5. Pearl has been invited to a Party.
6. Violet is going out Visiting.
7. Daisy is now at her Dressmaker's.
8. Winnie has just bought her winter Costumes.

Illustration 87-A pictures the cover of *Dolly's Dresses* showing one little girl seated and getting ready to dress one of her dolls. The other little girl has a paint brush in her hand. **Illustrations 87-B, C & D** picture three of the paper dolls mentioned above, complete with their costumes. Judging from the costumes shown, we suggest that this book dates between 1896 and 1901.

Truly a new and novel idea for the Tuck company appeared in the form of a trunk that opened up showing a paper doll and her costumes inside the trunk. There were four different sets in all, marked: "Dolly's Dainty Dresses," Series 1, 2, 3 and 4. The back of each trunk is marked with the easel and palette trademark,

"Raphael Tuck & Sons. Publishers to the Queen, London, Paris, New-York. Designed at the Studios in America. Printed in Bavaria." When the lid of the trunk is lifted, the inside reads as follows: "Dainty Doll Series U.S. Patent No. 534,824" and the number and the name of the doll. Series No. 1 is "Dolly Darling." She is marked with the easel and palette trademark, "By Special Appointment, Publishers to Her Majesty the Queen, Dolly Darling, Artistic Series No. 1. Patented. Designed at the Studios in America. Printed in Bavaria." The costumes have the same marking. We note here that a different United States patent number is used, perhaps for the style of the trunk. **(Illustration 88.)** "Dolly Darling" wears an ankle-length white chemise. Her paper trunk is on her left and her costumes below. Artistic Series 1 A is an ankle-length dress, green with pink flowers, a white collar and a pink ribbon sash. Artistic Series 1 B is an ankle-length coat dark blue with brown fur trim. Artistic Series 1 C is an ankle-length lavender overdress with dark purple trim and a soft yellow blouse. She holds a doll in her right hand. "Dainty Doll Series No. 2" is called "Dolly Dimple." This set is missing. "Dainty Doll Series No. 3" is called "Dolly Daisy." The doll and her costumes are marked in the same way as "Dolly Darling," except that they are marked: "Artistic Series No. 3." **Illustration 89** pictures "Dolly Daisy" standing next to her trunk. She is wearing a two-piece undergarment with lace trim. Her costumes reading from left to right are: Artistic Series 3 A is a green coat with a dark green cape collar trimmed with gray fur. She carries a matching muff with a pink ribbon trim. Artistic Series 3 B is a light blue dress with white polka dots; the large cape collar is dark blue and the underblouse is white. Artistic Series 3 C is a coral-colored dress with full sleeves and wide collar. She wears black gloves and stockings and carries a black fan. Her costumes are shorter in length than No. 1, indicating that she represents an older child. **Illustration 90** is called "Young America." This is a young boy who is marked the same as the previous dolls except that he is Artistic Series No. 4. He stands to the right of his trunk and his only remaining costume is to the left. He is wearing a two-piece light blue suit and black stockings. His dark green coat, trimmed with brown fur, is marked: "Artistic Series No. 4." He carries a pair of skates and wears long brown leggings buttoned on the side.

The volume of published material during the reign of Queen Victoria was tremendous and we have attempted to provide as many objects for you as we possibly could. The next chapter will deal with the reign of King Edward and Queen Alexandra. This time period provides another large grouping of colorful paper toys, books and paper dolls to study.

Illustration 90. "Young America" with his trunk and one costume. He is marked: "Artistic Series No. 4." His one costume is marked: "Artistic Series No. 4 A." Trunk measures 7¼in x 5in (19cm x 13cm). Doll measures 6½in (17cm). Maurine Popp Collection.

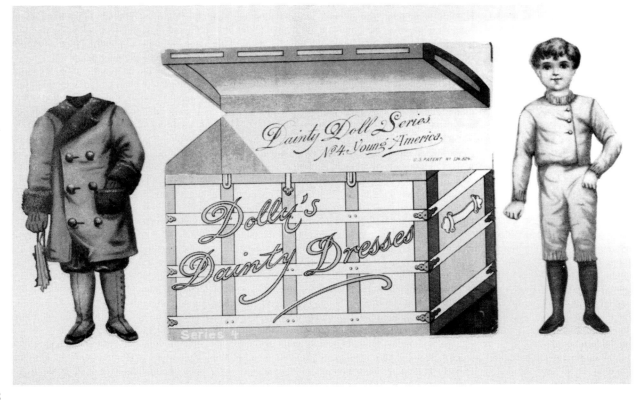

Color Illustration XIX-B. *The fourth set in the series of "The Belles of the Season Dressing Dolls." It is titled "Lady Lilian and Her Gowns." Top row, left to right we see "Visiting Costume, Artistic Series XIV-A," "Afternoon Gown, Artistic Series XIV-B," "Dinner Dress, Artistic Series XIV-C" and the lower row, left to right is "Lawn Tennis Costume, Artistic Series XIV-D," "In the Park, Artistic Series XIV-E" and "At the Ball, Artistic Series XIV-F." The costumes are marked with the easel and palette mark and "By Special Appointment, Publishers to Her Majesty the Queen, Raphael Tuck & Sons Ltd., London, Paris, New York, Designed at the Studios in England and Printed at the Fine Art Works in Bavaria." All are marked: "Copyright Patent No. 23,003, Artistic Series XIV."*

Color Illustration XX. *"Jolly Rover" is marked with the easel and palette mark and "Art Publishers by Royal Warrent, Patent, Raphael Tuck & Sons Ltd., London, Designed at the Studios in England and Printed at the Fine Art Works in Saxony." His costumes carry the same markings. The dog stands 8½in (21cm) tall. Maurine Popp Collection.*

Color Illustration XXI. *This colorful cat and her costumes are marked: "Art Publishers to Her Majesty, Patented, Designed at the Studios in England and Printed at the Fine Art Works in Saxony." The Tuck easel and palette trademark appears on all pieces. The cat is 8¼in (21cm) tall.*

Color Illustration XXII. A soldier on horseback with his various uniforms and equipment. The horseman is marked: "No. 37 A.B.C.D.E. and F., Raphael Tuck & Sons, London, Paris, New York, Art Publishers by Royal Warrent" and the easel and palette trademark. Each costume is marked: "No. 37" with one of the letters. The costumes carry the additional markings: "Designed at the Studios in England and Printed at the Fine Art Works in Saxony." The horseman is 13in high and the base is 12¼in wide (33cm by 31cm). Jean Woodcock Collection.

Color Illustration XXIII. This pictures a lovely paper doll with long blonde hair. The fence and each costume is marked with the easel and palette mark, also "Art Publishers by Royal Warrent, Raphael Tuck & Sons Ltd., London, Designed at the Studio in England and Printed at the Fine Art Works in Saxony." The doll measures 8½in (22cm) tall.

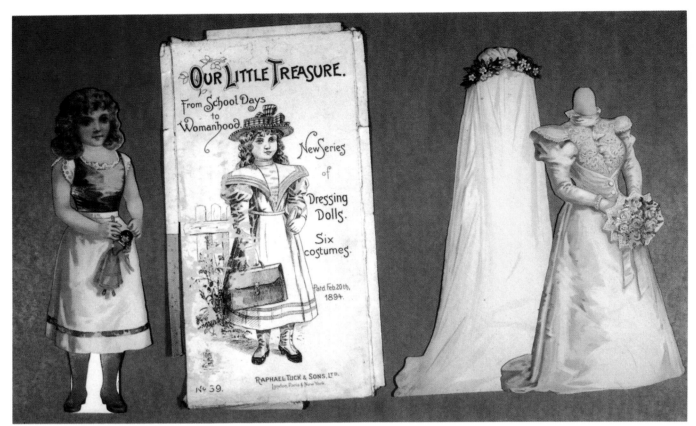

Color Illustration XXIV-A. *"Our Little Treasure" with her original box cover and bridal gown. The box cover, the doll and her costumes are marked with the Tuck easel and palette trademark and "Raphael Tuck & Sons Ltd., London, Paris, New York." The doll and costumes have the additional markings: "Designed at the Studios in England and Printed at the Fine Art Works in Saxony." Box cover measures 6¾in x 14in (17cm x 36cm). The doll measures 12½in (32cm) high. Maurine Popp Collection.*

Color Illustration XXIV-B. *Costumes for "Our Little Treasure" are marked similar to those in the preceding illustration. The five costumes reading from left to right are: the School Dress, Afternoon Dress, Evening Dress, Walking Dress, and finally, the traditional Mourning Dress. Maurine Popp Collection.*

Color Illustration XXV-A. *The original box cover for "Dear Dorothy, Artistic Series 500" with two of her dresses and hats. The cover reads as follows: "Dolls For All Seasons, Patented Feb. 20th, 1894, Dear Dorothy, Her Hats and Her Gowns, Designed by Margaret McDonald, Raphael Tuck & Sons, London, Paris, New York, Publishers to Her Majesty the Queen." Box cover measures 13in x 8½in (33cm x 22cm). Peggy Jo Rosamond Collection.*

Color Illustration XXV-B. *"Dear Dorothy" with two of her dresses and hats. All are marked with the easel and palette trademark and "By Special Appointment, Publishers to Her Majesty the Queen, Artistic Series 500, Patented, Raphael Tuck & Sons, London, Paris, New York, Designed in the Studios in New York and Printed at the Fine Art Works in Bavaria, U.S. Patent Feb. 20th, 1894, Copyright 1894 by Raphael Tuck & Sons Co., Ltd." Doll measures 13in (33cm). Peggy Jo Rosamond Collection.*

Chapter II

Part I

The Reign of King Edward and Queen Alexandra, 1901-1910

Puzzles, Postcards, Valentines and Children's Books.

Edward VII and Queen Alexandra reigned from 1901 to 1910 and all products produced by Raphael Tuck & Sons, Ltd., during that time period were marked: "Their Majesties, the King and Queen." The Tuck company had reached a high level of publishing in quality, quantity and variety at the turn-of-the-century. The intriguing paper toys, paper dolls and similar allied articles were carried over from Queen Victoria's time. New varieties of paper toys appeared, some with educational value, others were just plain fun. Also, there were wonderful paper dolls with wardrobes that colorfully spoke of the style changes in women's dress of the period.

Reverting back to the history of the company, in 1901 Raphael Tuck & Sons, Ltd., became a public company with an authorized capital of half a million pounds. The board of directors consisted of Adolph Tuck, Chairman and Managing Director, Gustave Tuck, Vice-Chairman and Director, Herman Tuck, Arthur Conan Doyle, M.D. and Alfred Parsons A.R.A. In the same years, Reginald and Desmond, sons of Adolph and Jeanette Tuck, joined the firm. In 1910, Adolph Tuck was created a baronet of the United Kingdom, becoming Sir Adolph Tuck.

The firm had now reached a position where its name was the hallmark of the highest quality in fine printing and publishing. Offered was a range of products, both wide and varied. While we will not delve into the varied branches of

Illustration 91. The cover of a 36-page catalog devoted entirely to puzzles. Pictured are over 100 puzzles, made in 17 sizes and consisting of 50 to 2000 pieces per puzzle. This catalog dates between 1901 and 1910 and size wise measures 7½in high and 5¼in wide (19cm x 13cm). Anne D. Williams Collection.

Illustration 92. *A boxed puzzle from "The Nation's Series" containing an Oilette Postcard picturing two military figures and a 36-piece puzzle identical to the card. The card is marked with the Tuck trademark and "The 2nd Life Guards, Raphael Tuck & Sons, Oilette Postcard No. 9426" and "Art Publishers to Their Majesties the King & Queen." The dark red box is 5in high, 6¾in wide and 3/4in deep (13cm x 17cm x 2cm).*

Illustration 93. *A half-page advertisement announcing an extensive new line of valentines for the year 1908. It was placed in Playthings, an American toy trade magazine. Size of advertisement, 4¼in high and 6½in wide. (11cm x 17cm).*

publishing that the firm was attending to during the early 1900s, one that should be mentioned in this writing is the publishing of puzzles. The puzzle production started about 1908 and lasted to about the beginning of World War II. They were published under the trade name, "Zag-Zaw." The first puzzles were backed with solid wood, the later ones were plywood. By the same token, the early puzzles did not interlock while the later ones did. **Illustration 91** pictures the cover of a Tuck catalog devoted entirely to their offerings of puzzles. Dating the catalog is rather difficult. You will notice the Tuck address at the bottom of the cover, "Raphael House, Moorfields, London, E.C." This building was opened in 1899. The words "Publishers to Their Majesties the King & Queen" suggests that the catalog was published between 1901 and 1910. It contains 36 pages, listing and picturing puzzles offered in 17 sizes. The Tuck firm produced a vast number of puzzles which are rather difficult to date accurately as they made use of some of the prints published in the 1880s.

As the Tuck firm had developed a massive variety of postcards, it seemed logical that they would develop a series of postcard puzzles. Tuck marketed the postcard puzzles, each consisting of 29 pieces, in sets of six puzzles. In this way the firm catered to the competitive contests. The flat mailing packet promoted their use for party games, where a number of guests could compete in a contest to see who could assemble their puzzle quickest.

A fine example of the "Zag-Zaw" puzzle mentioned above is a boxed set from "The Nation's Series." **(Illustration 92.)** It contains an Oilette Postcard picturing two distinguished members in dress uniform of the "2nd Life Guards Signallers" and a puzzle of 36 pieces identical to the card. An advertisement inside the box cover states the following information: "Tuck's Postcards, Christmas Cards, Calendars, Gift Books, Engravings, Toy Books, Painting Books and Birthday Books. Making History and Bringing Peace, Tuck's Postcard Exchange Register has been the means of cementing new and lasting friendships between thousands of postcard collectors all over the world. Catalog with listings of 75,000 Tuck Postcards sent post free on application. Raphael Tuck & Sons, Ltd., Raphael House, City London.''

At a point further on in this book, we will cover postcards that cover a number of paper dolls and paper toys that could be cut out and assembled. Also documented will be several series of postcards which picture two famous doll houses, their interior rooms and their furnishings. Valentines were another popular product published by Raphael Tuck & Sons, although their popularity never stayed at a high level. During the reign of King Edward, the fancy, possibly overdone lacy decoration of the pre-1900s was more or less gone. A new style, the large and beautiful mechanicals appeared and were readily accepted by the public. In 1908, Tuck apparently made an effort to attract the American market with a new line of valentines. A half-page advertisement appeared in the August 1908 issue of *Playthings* magazine, an American toy trade publication. It announced an extensive new and original line for 1908. Notice that an order could be submitted to either New York City or Montreal offices. **(Illustration 93.)**

A notice appearing in the same *Playthings* magazine stated that ''the valentine line published by Raphael Tuck & Sons in the past year was widely accepted by both the trade and the buying public. Early efforts have been surpassed in original designs, fresh and unique effects and artistic merit. An illustrated catalog is ready to be mailed out on application.'' In the same year, the November issue of *Playthings* offered a bit of information about the Tuck company under the section ''Trade Notes.'' ''Raphael Tuck & Sons have received notice that their exhibit at the Franco-British Exposition received the highest award, the Grand Prix. Their outstanding display of postcards, valentines, calendars and artistic novelties won for them this outstanding award.''

Some examples of Tuck valentines of this period are described as follows. A series of three lovely young ladies are dressed with oversize bonnets of the period and matching neck scarves done in beautiful soft colors. The scarves are mounted at the neck with a swivel pin. When the scarves are half rotated to cover the young ladies faces, a valentine message is revealed. **(Illustration 94.)** Another example, possibly made with the American market in mind, are the two mechanicals pictured in **Illustration 95**. These colorful die-cut embossed valentines, one in the form of a fashioned young lady of the day is marked: ''Fluffy Ruffles, Original Design Copyright 1907 by the New York Herald Co., All rights reserved.'' The second is a young man. This gentleman looks like he might be celebrating St. Patrick's Day, yet he carries a valentine message within a heart on his chest.

Further examples are offered in **Illustration 96** which pictures three smiling young people, each holding a package. By opening out the face of each package, a bouquet of colorful flowers is revealed. Each figure is equipped with a rear folding stand, enabling the figure to stand upright.

Illustration 94. Three die-cut valentines representing lovely young ladies with oversize bonnets and neck scarfs done in soft pastel colors. The scarfs are mounted at the neck with a swivel pin. When the scarf is half rotated, a message of love is revealed. Figures measure 7½in high and are 5¼in wide (19cm x 13cm). Grace Piemontesi Collection.

BELOW: Illustration 97. *A novel valentine fan done in soft warm colors. Marked on the back as follows: "Raphael Tuck & Sons, London, Paris, Berlin, New York, Montreal." Opened and extended, the fan measures 7in high and 12½in wide (18cm x 32cm).*

ABOVE: Illustration 96. *A group of young people in decorative dress, each holding a surprise package. Each figure is marked with the easel and palette trademark and "Raphael Tuck & Sons, Publishers to Their Majesties the King & Queen." Figures average 9in tall (23cm). Grace Piemontesi Collection.*

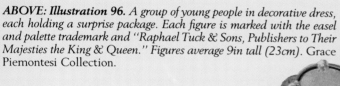

Illustration 95. *Two mechanical valentines with movement of the arms and legs motivated by a pull string, a form of Jumping Jack. The lady carries the easel and palette trademark and the words: "Raphael Tuck & Sons Ltd., Publishers by Appointment to Their Majesties the King and Queen, Printed in Germany." The male figure is unmarked but we attribute it to Tuck. The cardboard is of a similar weight and quality, the same embossing, identical brass fasteners and the same type of cord. Height of both figures 12¼in (31cm).*

A lovely valentine fan carries the following appropriate message: "Little Darling, The Flowers Bud and Bloom and Twine, Like you Round this fond heart of mine." **(Illustration 97.)** The background hearts are a soft red and frame the heads of the lovely children. The background color of the fan is peach and soft green with decorative gold lines intertwined between soft red bleeding hearts and pink roses. This delightful item would warm the heart of any young lady.

Juvenile books were an important part of the Tuck company production during this period and those that followed. An interesting and colorful example is titled *Our Friends at the Zoo, No. 609.* This little book features three highly-colored die-cut illustrations, parts of which pop out when the page is turned. Other titles in this series are *Robinson Crusoe, No. 604, Little Red Riding Hood, No. 605, The Three Bears, No. 606, The Three Kittens, No. 607* and *Fun At The Circus, No. 608.* The small hard cover book titled *Our Friends at the Zoo* consists of 16 pages. The story is about a group of six children who visit the zoo and the exciting time they had. The colorful illustrations picture the children entering the front gate of the zoo, a group of wild animals in their cages **(Illustration 98)**, and lastly, the children having a ride on the back of an elephant.

Illustration 98. Our Friends at the Zoo, No. 609 is a part of the "Combined Expanding Toys & Painting Book Series." It is marked with the easel and palette trademark and the following wording: "Raphael Tuck & Sons, London, Paris, New York, Designed at the Studios in England and Printed in Germany." Book size is 7in high and 5½in wide (18cm x 14cm).

Illustration 99. Two shape books with the same title, My Dolly, and the same "No. 2024." The one published in Britain is marked: "Raphael Tuck & Sons Ltd., London, Paris, Berlin, New York, Montreal, Publishers to Their Majesties the King & Queen." The second identical shape book is marked: "Raphael Tuck & Sons Co., Ltd., New York-London-Paris," with no reference to the Royal Family. Each book is 9½in high and 5⅛in wide (24cm x 13cm).

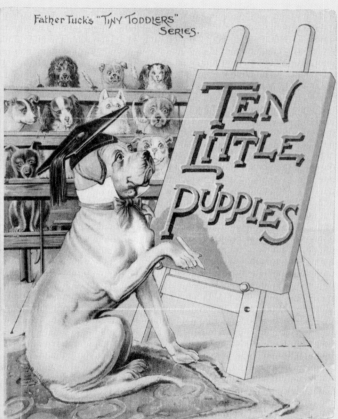

ABOVE: *Illustration 101.* Three ever popular juveniles published for the British market. All are part of "Father Tuck's Little Pets Series." Each is marked with the easel and palette trademark and "Raphael Tuck & Sons Ltd., London, Paris, Berlin, New York, Montreal, Art Publishers to Their Majesties The King & Queen, Designed at the Studios in England." Each measures 8⅞in high and 7in wide (23cm x 18cm).

LEFT: *Illustration 100.* A juvenile book titled Ten Little Puppies from Father Tuck's "Tiny Toddlers Series." It is marked with the Tuck trademark and "Raphael Tuck & sons Ltd., London, Paris, Berlin, New York, Montreal, Art Publishers to Their Majesties The King & Queen, Designed at the Studios in England." Size of book is 10¾in high and 8⅜in wide (27cm x 21cm).

RIGHT: *Illustration 102.* Four shape books published by Tuck for the American market, all from "Father Tuck's Doll Series." Each is marked with the easel and palette trademark and "Published by Raphael Tuck & Sons Co., Ltd., New York-London-Paris, Designed at the Studios in England." These shape books are 14⅝in in height and 7⅜in wide (37cm x 19cm).

The next two examples are from Father Tuck's "Doll Baby" series and "Sunny Days" series. Both are titled *My Dolly*. Both shape books are identical in size, shape, cover illustration, text and each has two interior color illustrations that are similar. The shape book on the left is the American version while the other was published for the British market. **(Illustration 99.)**

Ten Little Puppies is a highly amusing story of how ten young dogs came together and then, living through several adventurous events, disappeared one by one until just one remained. The title was from the "Tiny Toddlers" series. **(Illustration 100.)**

Pictured are three further examples of children's books, these from "Father Tuck's Little Pets" series. **(Illustration 101.)** Observe the numbers on these three examples, all of which are from the same time period. *Little Snow White*, No. 2334, *Little Red Riding Hood*, No. 7634 and *One, Two, Buckle My Shoe*, No. 7832. Observe the span of numbering. Remember, all these were published between 1901 and 1913. Other puzzling questions spring to mind when we find two identical *Mother Goose* picture books, a British edition and the other American. Both are marked: "Copyright 1904" and "1758." The differences are that the British version is marked: "London-Paris-Berlin-New York-Montreal" and "Publishers to Their Majesties The King & Queen." The American edition is marked: "New York-London-Paris" with no mention of the Royal Family. We have observed this before in other series, so we conclude that there may have been many other similar duplicate editions offered in both countries, each identical in copy and artwork, each having the same title and number.

One wonders how many of the large and colorful 14-page juvenile books were published by Tuck. Pictured are four large shape books from "Father Tuck's Doll Series," published for the American market. The ever popular shape book titled *Red Riding Hood*, No. 1467, tells the story in verse form. It contains seven color illustrations and 16 in black and white. *Dolly in the Country*, No. 1755, is a shape book with a cover picturing a child in an early dress of blue, heavily decorated with lace trim and a wide brim bonnet to match. She and the next two we will cover are similar in style to some of Tuck's early paper dolls issued during Queen Victoria's reign. The book contains eight color illustrations and 19 black and white line drawings. *Dolly in Town*, No. 1756, pictures a child in a lovely pink dress and

Illustration 103. Three shape books of varied subject matter, each from a different series. Beauty and the Beast, No. 4573 is from "Father Tuck's Happy Hour Series," Pussy's ABC, No. 1683 is from "Father Tuck's Christmas Series" and The Railroad ABC, No. 1757 is part of the "Father Tuck's Wide Awake Series." Each is marked with the Tuck trademark and "Raphael Tuck & Sons Co., Ltd., New York-London-Paris, Designed at the Studios in England." The Railroad ABC carries the additional marking "Copyright 1903." The books average 14⅛in tall and 7½in wide (36cm x 19cm).

bonnet. The stories are in verse form and are accompanied by nine color illustrations of children playing with their dolls. There are also 19 line drawings. *Dolly at Home*, No. 4571, still a shape book, pictures a child in a lavender dress and bonnet of the 1890 period on the cover. This book is similar in size and content to the two preceding shape books. This is an educational as well as an entertainment-type book with the copy in verse form. **(Illustration 102.)**

Three other large shape books published by Tuck for the American market have varied subject matter and are from a different series. *Beauty and the Beast* from "Father Tuck's Happy Hour Series" is one of the eternal favorite fairy tales. The story is of how Beauty became committed to the Beast, how he loved her and how she leaves for a trip and returns to find him lying on the ground. She falls to her knees and kisses the kind beast. This breaks a spell a witch had cast and the beast turns into a handsome Prince and they live happily ever after. The second book, *Pussy's ABC*, consists of short stories with cats as the story characters. This is an educational tool presented in such an amusing way that children find it entertaining to learn their ABCs. *The Railroad ABC* is very similar to the preceding book, but is definitely put together to gain the interest of boys. Train engines were of major interest to youngsters in the early 1900s. There was a fascination about the huge steam spouting monsters. It made sense to combine the interest with the learning of ABCs. **(Illustration 103.)**

"Father Tuck's Happy Hour Series" included *I'se Topsy, Happy Families ABC* and *Tales from Puppy Land*. How many other titles were offered in this series is unknown to us. Another question is posed; were some, or all of these books that were published for the American market also published for the British market? We have observed a few books that were produced for both markets, same title, copy and artwork, same number, but oddly enough not from the same series. **(Illustration 104.)**

Questions about the number of books in a series and the numbers of series published by Tuck becomes an insolvable puzzle at this point. Over the years we have collected these colorful picture books because we liked the interesting artwork. We admire both the Tuck and the McLoughlin books and a number of the more unusual examples published by lesser-known companies.

Illustration 104. Three titles from "Father Tuck's Happy Hour Series" which includes I'se Topsy! *No. 2049,* Happy Families ABC, *No. 2475 and* Tales from Puppy Land, *No. 2476. Each is marked with the Tuck trademark and "Published by Raphael Tuck & Sons Co., Ltd., New York-London-Paris, Designed at the Studios in England." They average 15in tall and 7½in wide (38cm x 19cm).*

Chapter II

Part II

The Reign of King Edward and Queen Alexandra, 1901-1910

Paper Toys of the Edwardian Period

The production of intriguing paper toys continued during the reign of Edward and Alexandra at the high level they had attained during Queen Victoria's time. How many different paper toys Raphael Tuck & Sons produced is unknown, but we will describe and picture a sampling of the many that we have collected, borrowed and observed over the years. The paper toys described within this book are not in numerical order although they are within their proper time period.

Pictured are two rather large die-cut figures of characters that will climb up a cord. The legs are connected to the figure's hips with a pivot pin, while a long cord is connected at the feet, hip and outstretched hands, all of which enable the figure to climb upward. Instructions printed on the back of each figure read: "Lower figure to the bottom of the cord. Hold or attach the top end of the cord to any suitable object, alternately pull and release the bottom end and the figure will climb upward. After the figure has reached the top, pull figure to bottom of cord and it will be ready to climb again." How many of these novelty climbing toys were produced by Tuck over the years is unknown to the authors. A listing of 12 figures was found in an early Gamage's toy catalog. The caption read as follows: "An excellent humorous and attractive novelty and a source of endless amusement." The 12 "Climbing Figures" are titled as follows: "Pretty Polly," "Highland Laddie," "Mr. Punch," "Our Pussy," "Our Doggie," "Beware of the Dog," "Jolly Jack Tar," "Little Billy," "Clown," "Teddy Bear," "Black Sambo" and "Monkey." **(Illustration 105.)**

A second group of toys that are activated by a pull cord are found in a box titled "Father Tuck's Marionettes." The original green box contains ten humorous figures with mechanical movement, each with a descriptive verse on the back by Clifton Bingham. **(Illustration 106-A.)** The ten characters are: "The Golliwogs and the Baby Wogs," "The Sailor Jolly Jack and His Teddy Bears," "Our Friends the Bears," "Dinah and Her Darlings," "Puss In Boots," "Dolly Daisy Dimple," "The Happy Jappy," "Bonnie Scotland," "Santa Claus" and "Red Riding Hood." **(Illustration 106-B.)** Each figure is jointed at the shoulder and each arm is connected to a downward pull cord which, when pulled, activates the arm to an up and down movement. The Clifton Bingham verse on the back of the Santa figure reads:

"Dear Old Santa Claus,
I'm Father Christmas as you see,
I know that you'll remember me.
I bring such presents, here's a pair,
I'm always welcome every where."
(Color Illustration XXVI.)

The following toys are those that have a rocking movement. "Father Tuck's Nursery Rockers" is the title of a boxed set of ten toyland characters. Pictured are three rockers with the following titles: "To and Fro" which are the bears in the forefront, "Off to the Party" and "Ups and Downs." **(Illustration 107-A.)** The other rocking characters in the set are "The Glad Golliwog," "The Bonnie Boatload," "The Three Little Kittens," "Mr. Jumbo," "The Game of Gallop," "Naughty" and "Tally-Ho!" Each of these paper toys is equipped with a back flap-type rocker which when spread, enables the figure to stand upright and with a

Illustration 105. These climbing action toys provided children with countless hours of amusement. With all the exercise they were given, it is surprising they have survived this long. Each figure is marked: "Publishers to Their Majesties the King & Queen" and "London, Paris, Berlin, New York, Montreal." These figures average 13in (33cm) high when extended.

ABOVE: Illustration 107-A. *Three rocking toys from a set titled "Father Tuck's Nursery Rockers." The bears in the forefront are titled "To and Fro," the others "Off to the Party" and "Ups and Downs." The back of each rocker is marked with the Tuck trademark and the following wording: "Raphael Tuck & Sons Ltd., Publishers to Their Majesties the King & Queen, London, Paris, Berlin, New York, Montreal, Designed in England, Printed in Bavaria." The three rockers average 7½in in height and 8½in in width (19cm x 22cm).*

BELOW: Illustration 106-B. *"The Friendly Bears" and "The Golliwogs" are two of ten figures found in a boxed set titled "Father Tuck's Marionettes." Each figure carries the Tuck trademark and the following wording: "Raphael Tuck & Sons Ltd., Publishers to Their Majesties the King & Queen, London, Paris, Berlin, New York, Montreal, Designed in England, Printed in Bavaria." Figures average 11¼in (29cm) in height.*

ABOVE: Illustration 106-A. *The box cover of "Father Tuck's Marionettes" has a green background. The illustrated cat and her kittens are white and red with a bit of green. The names of the ten marionettes are printed in white around the four sides of the cover. The box and cover measure 12in high, 7in wide and 1in deep (31cm x 18cm x 3cm).*

slight push, be made to rock. Printed on the back of each toy is either a four or eight line verse by Norman Gale. **Illustration 107-B** shows the red box cover of this beautifully colored and embossed set. The black and white illustration of the children on the rocking horse, pictured on the cover, is similar to one of the enclosed toys titled "A Game of Gallop."

A set of six rather large rocking animals representing a lion and a sheep, **(Illustration 108)**, a camel, a horse, an elephant and a cow. Each animal is well colored, deeply embossed, die-cut and is equipped with a hinged rear rocker which may be spread, enabling the animal to stand and be rocked. On the back of each

Illustration 107-B. Shown is the red box cover of a ten-piece set of colorful embossed rockers. The black and white illustration of the children on a rocking horse is similar to one of the toys in the set and is titled "A Game of Gallop." The box measures 8¾in high by 10in wide and 1in deep (22cm x 25cm x 3cm).

animal is the printed name or species of the animal in English and Latin. It is followed by an educational paragraph explaining the animals features and uses. An example: The Sheep (Ovis Domestica) is written up as follows: "The Sheep of our fields and downs is one of the most valuable possessions of the farmer. It is put to many useful purposes. The wool of its coat is woven into clothes of various kinds, its flesh is the mutton and the lamb that we eat, its fat is turned into tallow, and the skin is made into parchment. These animals vary considerably in size, from the small and black Kerry sheep of the south west of Ireland, to the large and white Southdown species."

"Father Tuck's Peep-Show Pictures of Fairy Tales," No. 9760, was another type of novelty toy that offered a source of boundless pleasure and provided hours of happy enjoyment to youngsters of the period. The reading of simple directions, cutting out the various parts, folding and sometimes pasting and finishing the toy brought about a feeling of satisfaction to the young builder. Each book consists of a beautiful colored cover and has six pages of charming pictures ready to be cut out and made into six attractive peep shows. Each has a front or face scene, a center scene and a back scene, three tiers deep. Although they are cleverly contrived, the construction is a simple matter. Instructions inside the front cover read "Detach the page and cut around the three pictures, the front, the center and the background scene. From the front and center cut away the white parts so that you can see through them. Carefully cut through the two short black lines on the background scene, so that there are slits. With a sharp pencil rule along the dotted lines on the front so that the side pictures will bend back more easily. Keep the color outside, and bend the side pictures straight back and into the slits which are cut in the side pictures, insert the tabs of the center picture, so that it goes across, color facing you. Fit the tabs on the side picture into the slits in the background scene and your Peep Show will stand up just like the children's on the cover of your book." **(Illustration 108.)** The peep show fairy tales include scenes from "Puss In Boots," "Rose-Red and Snow White," "The Three Bears," "Beauty and the Beast," "Sleeping Beauty" and "Cinderella." **Illustrations 109-A, B, C, D, E & F** picture the six uncut pages of the scenes mentioned above. When constructed, each peep show would measure 4in high, 4-3/8in wide and 2-1/2in deep (10cm x 11cm x 6cm).

Inside the back cover of the above "Peep Show Picture Book" is an advertisement about a second similar book. It reads "No. 9761, Father Tuck's Peep Show Pictures of Animals Wild and Tame." From this book can be made peep show scenes of animal life in farmland, and on the countryside, also in forest and jungle. All sorts of animals and birds being shown, admirably lifelike and all highly interesting and instructive." Another paper toy construction item mentioned on the same page was "No. 9762, Father Tuck's Toy Rockers Modelling Book, Patent No. 192306/22." The copy goes on: "A beautiful book full of delightful toys to be constructed by an extremely clever, patented, but simple device. There are seven pages of lovely designs of animals, dolls and other toys, which when cut out and made up, give 14 models of Rocking Horses, Rocking Boats, Rocking Chairs, etc. There are also little dollies to be cut out separately and put upon the rockers."

At this point we will turn from peep shows to panoramas. Tuck produced several fine examples of these toys during its long period of publishing. One fine example offered during Edward's reign was titled "With Father Tuck In Fairyland Panorama." **(Illustration 110-A.)** This was the standard type of folded panorama

Illustration 108. Two animals from a set of six or more rather large rocking animals. A second rocker at the rear of each animal may be spread, enabling the animal to stand. The back of each animal is marked with the easel and palette mark and the following wording: "Raphael Tuck & Sons Ltd., London-Paris-Berlin-New York-Montreal, Publishers to Their Majesties the King & Queen and TRH the Prince and Princess of Wales, Designed in England & Printed in Germany." Toys average 6¾in high and 8½in long (17cm x 22cm).

BELOW: *Illustration 109. The cover of "Father Tuck's Peep-Show Pictures of Fairy Tales" book. This construction book contains the parts to make six different three-tier peep shows. The back cover of the book pictures the Tuck trademark and the number "9760," also "Raphael Tuck & Sons, Ltd., Publishers to Their Majesties the King & Queen, London, Paris, New York, Designed in England — Printed in Bavaria." Booklet measures 8½in high and 10½in wide (22cm x 27cm).*

ABOVE: *Illustration 109-A. Pictured are three uncut pieces that make up the "Puss In Boots" peep show. No markings on object.*

Illustration 109-B. Three uncut pieces that make up the "Rose-Red and Snow-White" peep show. No markings.

Illustration 109-C. Three uncut sections of the peep show titled "The Three Bears." No markings.

with an added novelty feature. It consisted of four attached sections, each highly-colored section equipped with four or five short horizontal slits or pockets in which the die-cut story book characters could be inserted into the background, thereby forming a complete picture. Each section pictures a setting of such juvenile classics as "Red Riding Hood," "Sleeping Beauty," "Puss In Boots" and "Cinderella." **(Illustration 110-B.)** Included are two sections of flowing verses by Grace C. Floyd. Directions printed on back of the panorama read: "To make the Panorama Pictures, insert the figures, which will be found in the pocket attached to this book, into the spaces which are marked with numbers corresponding to those upon the figures. A variety of scenes, however, can be formed, and unending pleasure provided, by placing the figures in innumerable positions, and sometimes in one picture background sometimes in another, so that constant change and interest is obtained."

Another Tuck panorama from the same series as the preceding example is titled "With Father Tuck At The Seaside Panorama." It contains four folded

Illustration 109-D. Three uncut parts that make up the "Beauty and the Beast" peep show. No markings.

Illustration 109-F. Three uncut parts that make-up the "Cinderella" peep show. The above six sections are unmarked except for the title of each scene. When made up, each compact little peep show measures 4in high, 4⅜in wide and 2½in deep (10cm x 13cm x 6cm).

Illustration 109-E. Three uncut sections that make up the peep show titled "The Sleeping Beauty." No markings on any of the pieces.

sections, each picturing an interesting seaside view with young children at play. Each view is equipped with horizontal slits which accept the cut-out characters. The cover is pictured in **Illustration 111-A**, while **Illustrations 111-B & 111-C** picture two of the inner scenes.

Not a toy, but a paper base novelty, a Tuck product that provided amusement to children were the transfer pictures. Children were fascinated with this form of art. A single transfer was placed in a shallow saucer of water, soaked for a minute or two, then carefully lifted out of the water and placed color side down on a piece of paper, then lightly pressed with a cloth and then the final step of carefully sliding the paper off, leaving the color design on the paper. Boys usually transferred them to their arms to leave a tattoo of sorts. **Illustration 112** shows an open "Art Folio of Beautiful Transfer Pictures" and two strips of the transfers. "The Art Folios of Beautiful Transfer Pictures" were offered in the following series.

Series 1. Flowers, Fruits, Butterflies, Insects.
Series 2. Birds and Animals.
Series 3. Birds, Beasts, Fishes, Reptiles.
Series 4. Butterflies, Small Flowers and Fruit.

Illustration 113 pictures the folder cover of "Father Tuck's Little People Transfer Pictures" titled "Chubby Children" from the 704 series. There were 12 different titled folders in this series, all uniform in size and price. The "Chubby Children" folder pictured contains folded strips containing 15 transfers pictures of chubby youngsters with instructions printed on the inside front cover.

The fact that children are nearly always intrigued with animals must have inspired Tuck to publish this set of wild and domestic beasts. **(Illustration 114.)** On the back of each animal is a paragraph stating its importance to man. The pig (Sus) says: "The domestic pig, with which we are familiar, is of the greatest use to man. His flesh when cured is called bacon, and when fresh is called pork. Pig skin is used for making the strongest leather, while the bristles of the coat are made into brushes. In the country of England, pigs are kept in enormous quantities by the rich farmer, and even the humble peasant often can boast of one or two hogs in his sty." "The Lion (Felis Leo) is called the King of Beasts, and is one of the most powerful of the Cat tribe. It is to be found in Africa, Persia and India, although in the last named country it is becoming very scarce. The male Lion differs from all other members of the Cat family on account of the great mane that covers the head, neck and shoulders, and the tuft at the tip of the tail in which is a small claw."

We have previously mentioned that the Tuck company had produced a large number of puzzles, but the majority of them were mainly for adults or older

ABOVE LEFT: Illustration 110-A. The cover of the book With Father Tuck In Fairyland Panorama. *The back cover of the book is marked with the Tuck trademark and "No. 8598." Other markings are as follows: "Raphael Tuck & Sons, Ltd., Publishers to Their Majesties the King & Queen, London, Paris, New York, Designed in England, Printed in Bavaria." Opened out the panorama measures 47½in long and is 10½in high (120cm x 27cm).*

ABOVE: Illustration 110-B. One section of the "With Father Tuck In Fairyland Panorama" titled "Cinderella." The inserted figures represent the Prince on the left, one of the Stepsisters at the rear, the Fairy in the lower front and Cinderella. No markings. Section measures 10½in high and 12in wide (27cm x 35cm).

Illustration 111-A. Titled "With Father Tuck At the Seaside Panorama" is similar in style to the preceding "With Father Tuck In Fairyland Panorama." It is marked with the easel and palette trademark and "No. 8598," also "Raphael Tuck & Sons, Ltd., Publishers to Their Majesties the King & Queen, London-Paris-New York, Designed in England, Printed in Bavaria." Size 10½in x 12in (27cm x 35cm).

LEFT: Illustration 111-B. A scene from the "With Father Tuck At The Seaside Panorama." The five children are inserted in three horizontal slots. No markings. Size 10½in x 12in (27cm x 35cm).

BELOW: Illustration 111-C. A scene from the "With Father Tuck At The Seaside Panorama." The two children in the forefront and the three in the boat are inserted figures placed in horizontal slots. No markings. Size is 10½in x 12in (27cm x 35cm).

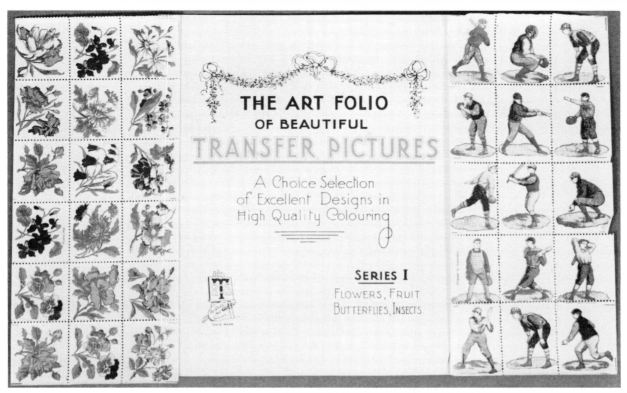

ABOVE: Illustration 112. An open "Art Folio of Beautiful Transfer Pictures" and two strips of colored transfers. The folder carries the Tuck trademark on its cover along with the title and the series number. The back of the folder is marked: "Raphael Tuck & Sons, Ltd., Publishers to Their Majesties the King & Queen, London, Paris, New York, Printed in Bavaria." Folio size folded is 8⅝in high by 7¼in wide (22cm x 18cm). The transfers came in a variety of small sizes, the largest being 1¾in square (5cm).

RIGHT: Illustration 113. "Father Tuck's Little People Transfer Pictures." Back of folder is marked: "Raphael Tuck & Sons, Ltd., London-Paris-New York," and stamped: "Printed in Germany." It is also marked with the easel and palette trademark. Size 4⅜in x 6½in (11cm x 17cm).

Illustration 114. Pictured are two animals, a pig and a lion. On the back of each is information concerning their importance to man. They are also marked with the Tuck easel and palette mark and "Publishers to Their Majesties the King and Queen, Raphael Tuck & Sons Ltd., London, Paris, Berlin, New York, Montreal." Animals average 10in (25cm) in length.

Illustration 115-A. The box cover of "Father Tuck's Picture-Building A.B.C." and one of the three puzzles which make up the set. The puzzle illustrates the popular "Red Riding Hood." The cover is marked: "Publishers to Their Majesties the King and Queen, London, Paris, Berlin, New York & Montreal, Designed in England — Printed in Holland." Notice the "Printed in Holland." Box measures 10³⁄₄in high, 8³⁄₄in wide and ¹⁄₂in deep (27cm x 22cm x 1cm). Each puzzle is 10¹⁄₂in x 8¹⁄₂in (27cm x 22cm).

Illustration 115-B. British patent drawing for the type of puzzle titled "Father Tuck's Picture-Building A.B.C." and "Patent No. 4665," dated "Feb. 25, 1909." Issued to Albert Ernest Kennedy.

children. This next puzzle titled "Father Tuck's Picture-Building A.B.C." is geared for smaller children. **(Illustration 115-A.)** This boxed set contains three old favorite story book puzzles, "Red Riding Hood," "Cinderella" and "Robinson Crusoe." Each puzzle, when taken apart, contains the 26 letters of the alphabet which can again be built up to form a complete picture. The back of each puzzle tray has a condensed story version of the scene on the face of the completed puzzle. And while the story of little Red Riding Hood seems to have several different kinds of endings, this one was a happy one. The last few sentences read: "But, Grannie, what big teeth you have! said Red Riding Hood. She was really getting quite frightened. The better to eat you up! said the wolf, and he sprang from the bed, but just in time, Red Riding Hood's father ran in, and killed him, and just fancy it, when he was cut open, why, out stepped the Grannie, quite hale and hearty. So everything ended happily after all." Each puzzle was also marked: "Patent No. 4665 of 1909." This is one of the few Tuck toys that was dated **(Illustration 115-B)** that pictures the original patent drawing.

Another set of ABCs that must be considered an educational toy that is geared for the younger set is colorful, die-cut and embossed. There is a simple verse along the bottom of the two-section card; it has the letter on the left half and an appropriate illustration on the right. **Illustration 116** pictures cards A and B.

Illustration 117 pictures two of Tuck's colorful cardboard doll houses that were advertised in the March 1910 issue of the American toy trade magazine *Playthings.* "Little Pets' Doll House" is a two-story affair measuring 17in (43cm) high. Along with the house were four sheets of dolls, each sheet containing a doll with six dresses and six hats. The second house, "Home Sweet Home" was accompanied by two sheets of furniture. "Home Sweet Home" is pictured on the back of a large three-part folder. This illustration pictures what seems to be a rather large cardboard house, while the toy itself is a two room affair. The three-part folder forms the ceiling, back wall and floor. **Illustration 118-A** pictures a drawing of the exterior of the house. **Illustration 118-B** shows the interior two rooms. The pink parlor on the left has a curtained opening on the left wall revealing a dining room and a double door at the rear wall which reveals a horseless carriage outside. A doorway on the right wall leads revealing outside views. The open door on the right wall reveals a bathroom. **Illustration 118-C** shows an uncut card of parlor furniture consisting of 12 pieces. **Illustration 118-D** displays the second uncut card, a bedroom set, consisting of 11 pieces of furniture. Both furniture cards are marked with similar directions: "Score on the dotted lines; bend parts down, back or up, as may be necessary, and paste on to the yellow tabs."

Tuck's toys are marked: "Publishers to Their Majesties the King and Queen and T.R.H. the Prince and Princess of Wales" and are also marked with cities including "Montreal" included within the time frame of the reign of Edward and Alexandra.

Illustration 119-A pictures a box cover titled "Father Tuck's Patent Walking Animals" which contains six different domestic animals. The animals represent a lamb and a donkey, pictured in **Illustration 119-B**, also a dog, cat, cow and a rabbit, making up the balance of the set. Each animal is die-cut, embossed, two-sided,

A for the Apples
so rosy and red,

One for you, one for me,
one for good Ted.

B for the Baby
who sits in the chair,

He'll lose his small shoe
if he doesn't take care.

ABOVE: *Illustration 116. A striking series of alphabet die-cut and embossed letters accompanied by a colorful object relative to the letter and a verse along the bottom of the two-section card. Only the card marked: "A" is marked with the easel and palette trademark. It is also marked: "No. 2520, Raphael Tuck & Sons Ltd., London-Paris-New York, Designed in England, Printed in Germany." Size per double unit, 4½in high by 6in wide (11cm x 15cm).*

Illustration 117. "Tuck's Doll Houses" was the title on a full-page advertisement that appeared in the March 1910 issue of the American toy trade magazine Playthings. *Page size 10½in x 7½in (27cm x 19cm).*

113

Illustration 118-A. Pictured is "Home Sweet Home For Dainty Dollies" printed on the back of a three-section card folder which forms the floor, back wall and ceiling of the two rooms shown in the next illustration. Back is marked with Tuck trademark and "Raphael Tuck & Sons Co., Ltd., London, Paris, Berlin, New York, Montreal, Copyrighted." Folded, the folder is 8in high and 14in wide (20cm x 36cm).

Illustration 118-B. Shown are the two rooms when set up, the pink-walled parlor on the left and the blue bedroom on the right. Together the two rooms measure 7¼in high, 12½in wide and 6in deep (18cm x 32cm x 15cm).

Illustration 118-C. An uncut card of parlor furniture to be cut out and glued together. Furniture is scaled about ½in (1cm) to a foot (31cm). Card size 7½in high by 11½in wide (19cm x 29cm).

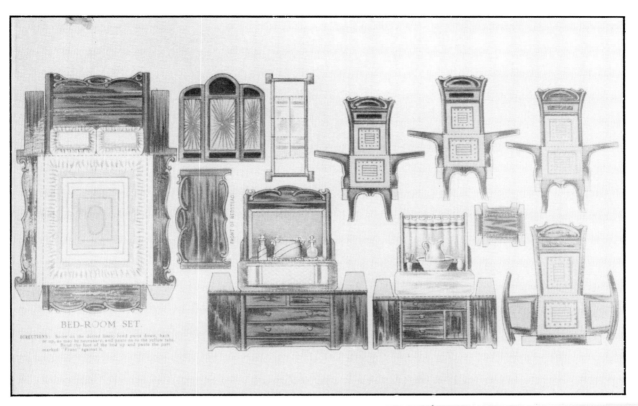

ABOVE: Illustration 118-D. *Uncut card titled "Bed Room Set," which when cut out and assembled would complete the furnishing of the two room cottage "Home Sweet Home For Dainty Dollies." Card size 7½in high by 11½in wide (19cm x 29cm).*

Illustration 119-A. *The box top of "Father Tuck's Patent Walking Animals" and the young lady who can be positioned to ride on the backs of the various animals. The back of the little girl is marked with the Tuck trademark, also "Raphael Tuck & Sons, Ltd., London-Paris-Berlin-New York-Montreal, Designed in England & Printed in Saxony, Publishers to Their Majesties the King & Queen and T.R.H. the Prince & Princess of Wales." The box measures 6½in high, 8½in wide and 1⅜in deep (17cm x 22cm x 4cm).*

ABOVE: Illustration 119-B. *Two of Tuck's patented walking animals. Animals are all marked as in the caption of Illustration 119-A. They are also marked: "United Kingdom Patent 9117 of 1909" and "United States Patent applied for." The lamb is 6in by 8in (15cm x 20cm) which is the average size of each animal.*

115

ABOVE: Illustration 120. A boxed set titled "Father Tuck's Rocking Animals." Pictured are two of the ten rocking animals in the set. All are marked with the easel and palette mark and "Raphael Tuck & Sons, Ltd., London-Paris-Berlin-New York-Montreal, Publishers to Their Majesties the King & Queen and T.R.H. the Prince and Princess of Wales, Designed in England & Printed in Germany." The red box is 8in high, 9¼in wide and 1in deep (20cm x 24cm x 3cm). The elephant is 8in tall and 9in long (20cm x 23cm).

Illustration 121-A. The box cover of "Father Tuck's Mechanical Birds" set of "Series 8, Feathered Friends." Inside of cover lists and names the various series available. The box measures 6¾in high, 10¼in wide and 1¼in deep (17cm x 26cm x 3cm).

LEFT: Illustration 121-B. The six birds of the set titled "Father Tuck's Mechanical Birds." They are marked: "Raphael Tuck & Sons, Ltd., London, Paris, Berlin, New York, Montreal, Publishers to Their Majesties the King & Queen and T.R.H. the Prince and Princess of Wales, Designed in England & Printed in Germany." Each bird is also marked: "Patented in England, France, Germany & America." Average height of standing birds is 8in (20cm).

folded along the top and open at the bottom, tent shape. Each is made in two sections, jointed loosely above the hips. A cord is fastened at the top of the head. When pulled forward and upward slowly, the beast will walk and move forward in a somewhat lifelike manner. A small girl positioned in a sitting position and holding a small whip is included in the set. She may be placed on the back of any of the animals and taken for a ride. An educational feature is printed on the back side of each animal. The gender of each animal is also named in both English and Latin. An added caption tells of its uses as a domestic animal and its qualities in the wild.

Another set of popular animal figures was titled "Father Tuck's Rocking Animals." The red box contains ten die-cut animals on rockers. These realistically colored and embossed animals are colored on one side only and have a second rocker hinged horizontally at the back of the animal so that when spread, will stand upright and rock back and forth. The elephant and tiger are pictured. **(Illustration 120.)** The other animals represented are a camel, cat, dog, horse, cow, donkey, lion and a sheep. Each animal is titled in English and Latin. Each has a caption of educational value regarding the animal. The elephant caption reads as follows: "One of the largest of animals, the Elephant is also one of the most intelligent. Even when caught in a wild state, it is easily tamed and can be trained to become most useful. It can pull the heavy guns of the Artillery in India, or pile in correct order heavy logs. Elephants are found in Africa and India, the African species being much

Illustration 122-A. The box cover of "Father Tuck's Mechanical Animals" set of "Series 5, 6 Pet Dogs." The inside cover lists the various sets in the series. The box measures 6¾in high, 10¼in wide and 1¼in deep (17cm x 26cm x 3cm). Maurine Popp Collection.

Illustration 122-B. Two of the dogs equipped with the patented joints which enable them to be placed in several different lifelike positions. Each dog is marked: "Raphael Tuck & Sons, Ltd., London, Paris, Berlin, New York, Montreal, Publishers to Their Majesties the King & Queen, designed in England & Printed in Germany." Each is also marked: "Patented in England, France, Germany, & America." Average height of dogs is 4½in (11cm). Maurnee Popp Collection.

Illustration 122-C. Pictures two of the six dogs from the set "Father Tuck's Mechanical Animals, Series 5." Markings and height of dogs are identical to those pictured in Illustration 122-B. Maurine Popp Collection.

Illustration 122-D. Two of the dogs from the set titled "Father Tuck's Mechanical Animals, Series 5, 6 Pet Dogs." Markings and height of dogs are identical to those shown in Illustrations 122-B & C. Maurine Popp Collection.

the bigger of the two, and also having larger ears than their Indian brothers. The species here illustrated is the Indian kind."

Turning from domestic and wild animals to birds, we find a boxed set titled "Father Tuck's Mechanical Birds," Series 8. **(Illustration 121-A.)** Inside the box cover are listings of animals in each of the eight series or boxed sets.

Series I. Contains six Domestic Animals.
Series II. Six Wild & Tame Animals.
Series III. Features six Wild Animals.
Series IV. Features six Assorted Animals.
Series V. & VI. Are not accounted for.
Series VII. Contains six Friends at the Farm.
Series VIII. Contains the six Feathered Friends Pictured in **Illustration 121-B**. The various birds pictured left to right and downward are a jay, cockatoo, parrot, owl, pheasant and a peacock. On the reverse side of each bird is its name in English and Latin along with a short paragraph giving educational information about the bird, where it originated, its habitat, and so forth. The circular moving joint in the neck, tail and legs is unusual and patented in England, France, Germany and the United States. While the patented joint is rather simple in structure, an explanation of it is not. Basically, it consists of five-sixth circumference of a 3/4in (2cm) circle die-cut into the leg of a bird. The remaining uncut one-sixth serves as a connection holding the nearly round tab that was cut out. This round tab is then inserted into a smaller 3/8in (.9cm) hole in the lower body of the bird. Naturally, the larger tab has to be curled to fit into the smaller hole. Once inserted, the tab is flattened out. All this is done using a rather heavy stiff cardboard.

A companion set to "Father Tuck's Mechanical Birds" is titled "Father Tuck's Mechanical Animals, 6 Pet Dogs." **(Illustration 122-A.)** The same patented joints used in the previous set is used on the various dogs in this set. Five patented joints are used on each animal. One on the shoulder area controls the positioning of the dog's head; the other four are located at the upper part of the thigh of each leg, offering movement to each leg. **(Illustrations 122-B, C & D.)**

During this period, Tuck offered a series of six or more tiny folding room settings which pictured outstanding detail in a small scale. Colorful die-cut settings, folded and held in place with tabs, they formed three walls and floored rooms that are equipped with hinged furniture and/or figures. A ballroom pictures a mother playing a piano and her eldest son playing a violin, while several children danced in a party-like atmosphere. Another room, the dining room, pictures children playing with a doll and a doll house on a table while a fourth child takes a doll out of a cradle. **Color Illustration XXVII-A** pictures a kitchen scene where a cook and a maid are preparing food. A small child stands nearby and looks on. A fourth room is that of a drawing room which is fitted with Edwardian furniture. The father sits in a wicker armchair reading a newspaper. The mother reads a story to her small son and daughter. The family is enjoying an evening together in front of the fireplace. **Color Illustration XXVII-B** pictures the bathroom in which two children are shown bathing in the tub while a third one is being bathed in a table tub by a governess. **Color Illustration XXVII-C** shows a nursery scene where the children are being put in bed for a good night's sleep.

Chapter II

Part III

The Reign of King Edward and Queen Alexandra, 1901-1910
Stylish Paper Dolls and Their Fashionable Costumes

The House of Tuck continued to publish a variety of wonderful paper dolls during this 1901-1910 period. The paper doll costumes published represented the high style of the period, the use of bright contrasting colors, wide flaring collars on coats and wide-brimmed head wear decorated with either oversized flowing plumed feathers or a seemingly over abundance of flowers. Dresses featured puffed shoulders and the use of ribbon bows. These design characteristics appeared in the costumes of the young ladies as well as those of the adults where the emphasis was placed on thin waistlines. Raphael Tuck & Sons kept up with current changing fashions, much to the delight of the children of the Edwardian period and to the pleasure of today's collectors.

The following paper doll is called "Darling Muriel," No. 23 and is a set from the "Little Darling Series of Dressing Dolls." **(Illustration 123.)** This series was also published during the Victorian period under the same series name, but with different numbers. See *Illustration 80* in the previous chapter. This doll has long blonde hair covering her shoulders and has the unusual feature of two horizontal slots on the hair at each shoulder to accept the dress shoulder tabs. She wears a light blue chemise trimmed with white lace around the short sleeves and the neckline. She also wears a thin white sash around her waist. Her first outfit is marked: "No. 23-A" and consists of a purple knee-length dress, a white hip-length coat with an extremely wide double collar and leg-o-mutton sleeves; the lining is purple. She wears tan leggings and gloves, purple shoes and an oversize hat to match, decorated with purple plumes and three white bows. Costume No. 23-B consists of a knee-length red dress and a three-tier shoulder cape of white, red and white. Her leggings are tan and she has white shoes. Her broad-brimmed white hat has a red feathery plume and a large red and white striped bow. Costume No. 23-C is a pink

Illustration 123. A doll marked: "Darling Muriel No. 23 of the Little Darling Series of Dressing Dolls." Also marked with the Raphael Tuck easel and palette trademark, "Publishers by Appointment to Their Majesties the King and Queen. Raphael Tuck & Sons Ltd., London, Paris, New York. Printed at the Fine Art Works in Bavaria." Same doll as Illustration 80, but has two horizontal slots on the hair at each shoulder to accept the dress shoulder tabs. Doll measures 9in (23cm).

23-A.   23-C.   23-D.   23-B.

Illustration 124. *"The Bride" printed on an uncut sheet from "The Bridal Party Series." Also pictured is the cover of the original box from "Father Tuck's Doll Sheets." This box lists the four series included in this set, "Children From Many Lands," "Bridal Party," "Little Pets" and "Fairy Tales." Box measures 18½in x 10½in (47cm x 26cm). Doll sheet measures 17½in x 9in (45cm x 23cm).*

Illustration 125-A. *The original envelope for "Children From Many Lands," Series No. 1, designed by Frances Brundage. Envelope measures 9½in x 5½in (24cm x 14cm). Doll measures 8½in (22cm).*

knee-length dress with a broad three-tier white cape that has a pink lining. The broad-brimmed pink hat features a red bow and two large white plumes. Her lower legs are covered with tan button-up leggings and white shoes. The last outfit is costume No. 23-D. It is a green hip-length coat with leg-o-mutton sleeves and yellow trim. Her knee-length skirt and leggings are white. Her shoes are yellow. The broad-brimmed hat is white decorated with a large yellow and green double bow and a flowing yellow feather.

Using many dolls that first appeared during the reign of Queen Victoria, Raphael Tuck & Sons published "Father Tuck's Doll Sheets." Each sheet was marked with the Tuck easel and palette trademark, "Publishers to Their Majesties the King and Queen. Raphael Tuck & Sons Ltd. London, Paris, Berlin, New York and Montreal. Printed in Germany." However, none of these markings appeared on the dolls or their costumes, just on the uncut sheets. This made it difficult to identify the dolls and their costumes after they were cut out. **Illustration 124** pictures an original box and one of the paper doll sheets from this set. The box is brown with black and red printing. It contains eight uncut sheets of paper dolls from four series. They are: "Children From Many Lands," "Bridal Party," "Little Pets" and "Fairy Tales."

A series that could have appeared first during the Reign of Queen Victoria, but one that we feel fits into the Reign of King Edward and Queen Alexandra is "Children From Many Lands," New and Instructive Series of Dressing Dolls. The usual reference to the reigning royalty does not appear on this series, making it difficult to determine where it belongs time wise. Series No. 1 represents costumes from England, Scotland, Wales and Ireland. The original brown paper envelope and the doll with her costumes is shown in **Illustrations 125-A & 125-B.** The original brown envelope is marked as follows: "Children From Many Lands. New and Instructive Series of Dressing Dolls." The easel and palette trademark is pictured, also "Published by Raphael Tuck & Sons Co. Ltd. New York and designed by Frances Brundage." The doll and her costumes are unmarked. The blonde-haired doll is wearing a two-piece white chemise and her four costumes represent England, Scotland, Wales and Ireland as we have mentioned before. Series No. 2 represents Italy, Indian, Japan and Turkey. Series No. 3 represents Germany, Alcase, Canada and Holland. We have not found that a Series No. 4 was published but because so many of the Tuck series appeared in sets of four, we feel that No. 4 is feasible. Also, it is conceivable that a fourth set would contain a costume from the United States because the Tuck company issued this series from New York.

We have mentioned before that Raphael Tuck & Sons were very careful to mark and identify most of their paper dolls. During the reign of King Edward and Queen Alexandra, this procedure changed somewhat. Many more of the series published at this time came with very little identification. If you have the original box or envelope, that could be of great assistance to you in your research but without them, it is sometimes difficult to identify the objects.

Illustration 126 pictures four box covers from the "Little Maids New Series of Dressing Dolls." This series consists of "Sunny Susan, No. 41," "Serene Sybil, No. 42," "Playful Polly, No. 43" and "Fair Frances, No. 44." All four of these paper dolls and their costumes are unmarked as to their names and numbers.

"Sunny Susan, No. 41" is a paper doll representing a young girl with dark brown hair. She is dressed in a white chemise decorated with lavender bows. Her four costumes include two long dresses, a play dress and an outfit with a coat, muff and leggings. All the costumes have hats to match. **(Color Illustration XXVIII.)**

"Serene Sybil" is a paper doll with blonde hair falling to her shoulders. She wears a blue bow in her hair and has a blue and white chemise with pink bows along the neckline and a pink sash around her waist. She has four costumes with matching hats, a tan coat, plaid skirt and high laced shoes, a peasant dress, a long afternoon dress and a rather formal dark dress with high walking boots. **(Color Illustration XXVIX.)**

LEFT: Illustration 125-B. A blonde-haired doll with her four costumes. The upper left represents Scotland, upper right Wales, lower left Ireland and lower right England. Doll measures 8½in (22cm).

BELOW: Illustration 126. Four box covers from the "Little Maids New Series of Dressing Dolls," "Sunny Susan No. 41," "Serene Sybil No. 42," "Playful Polly No. 43" and "Fair Frances No. 44." All are marked with the easel and palette trademark and "Raphael Tuck & Sons Co., Ltd., London, Paris, New York. Publishers by Appointment to Their Majesties the King and Queen Alexandra." Box cover measures 13in x 9in (33cm x 23cm). Maurine Popp Collection.

Illustration 127. The original cover, the paper doll and three of her costumes for "The Little Darlings New Series of Dressing Dolls, Artful Alice." The cover is marked: "Raphael Tuck & Sons Ltd. London, Paris, Berlin, New York, Montreal. Patented Feb. 20th 1894. Art Publishers to Their Majesties the King and Queen." The doll and her costumes read: "Published by Appointment to Their Majesties the King and Queen. Patd. Feb. 20th, 1894. Raphael Tuck & Sons Ltd. London, Paris, Berlin, New York and Montreal. Designed at the Studios in New York and printed at the Fine Art Works in Saxony." Box measures 13½in x 9in (35cm x 23cm). Doll measures 13in (33cm). Maurine Popp Collection.

The third paper doll in this "Little Maids New Series of Dressing Dolls" is titled "Playful Polly." She has a lavender bow in her blonde hair. She wears a lavender chemise with a red ribbon bow threaded through a white collar, a red sash around her waist and a double gathered yellow fringe along the lower part of the skirt. Her four costumes consist of a dark velvet coat with fur trim, a green and red party dress with a wide pink collar, a youthful dress holding a doll in her arm and a school dress consisting of a plaid cape-like jacket and a tan skirt. **(Color Illustrations XXX-A, B & C.)**

The last set in this series is titled "Fair Frances." She is a brunette with a thin yellow bow in her hair. She wears an off-white chemise with pink trim. Her four costumes include a deep yellow dress and she holds a doll and a fan in her arms. Another costume is a long blue school dress with a school bag, an ankle-length dress and afternoon dress with a sun umbrella. All the costumes have appropriate head wear. **(Color Illustration XXXI.)**

This concludes the "Little Maids New Series of Dressing Dolls," but we would like to elaborate further on the fact that these dolls and their costumes are not numbered or named. The Raphael Tuck & Sons is there, but very little else. When four dolls such as these appear in their original boxes, we have to assume that this is correct. Some collectors may say that their sets differ. This is possible. Over the years it stands to reason that some dolls and costumes may have been switched but we feel that these "Little Maids" are pictured and listed in a logical way.

Illustration 127 pictures "Artful Alice" with her original box cover and three of her costumes. This is from the "Little Darlings New Series of Dressing Dolls." This is another paper doll that is unmarked as to name and number but the cover helps to identify her. She wears a pale green chemise with a darker green floral print in the fabric. Her stockings are also green. Her short red hair is complimented by two lavender ribbon bows. Her three costumes are pictured on the top row. From left to right, we see her blue coat with a white collar and cuffs trimmed in blue. She has brown gloves and a red handbag. Her second costume is a lovely white party dress trimmed with lace and green ribbon. She is wearing long beige gloves and holds a red book in her right hand. Her left hand holds a handkerchief. The third costume is a red dress with a red hip-length coat that has a wide white collar trimmed with red dots. She is carrying a pail and shovel. Her fourth costume is missing.

Two other dolls that we feel are part of the "Little Darlings" series are described next. The first is another redhead similar to "Artful Alice." She is wearing a white chemise top with a red corset over it. Her petticoat is green and trimmed with lace. She holds a hairbrush in her right hand and a blue ribbon in her left. Her stockings are purple and she wears red shoes. From left to right, her first costume is a soft blue and is trimmed with white lace. Her stockings are dark blue and her brown shoes have blue bows. She is holding a doll in her arms who is wearing a green polka dot dress and has a red hat, sash and shoes. The second costume is a dark green coat over a purple dress. There is a pale lavender ribbon tied

Color Illustration XXVI. "Santa Claus," a marionette from the boxed set "Father Tuck's Marionettes." He holds a black clown doll in one hand and a doll dressed in blue in the other. The marionette is marked with the easel and palette trademark and "Raphael Tuck & Sons Ltd. Publishers to Their Majesties the King and Queen, London, Paris, Berlin, New York and Montreal. Designed in England and Printed in Bavaria." The Santa Claus figure measures 11½in (29cm). Herbert Hosmer Collection.

Color Illustration XXVII-A. A colorful tiny card model of a kitchen scene, typical of those found in the fine homes during the Edwardian Period in England. Marked with the Tuck trademark and "Raphael Tuck & Sons Ltd., London, Paris, New York. Publishers by Appointment to Their Majesties the King and Queen Alexandra. Printed in Germany." Size when assembled is 2½in high, 4in wide and 1¾in deep (6cm x 10cm x 4cm).

Color Illustration XXVII-B. *Bath night for children in the Edwardian home. The back of the scene is marked with the Tuck trademark and "Raphael Tuck & Sons Ltd., London, Paris and New York. Publishers by Appointment to Their Majesties the King and Queen Alexandra. Printed in Germany." Assembled size is 2½in high, 4in wide and 1¾in deep (6cm x 10cm x 4cm).*

ABOVE LEFT: Color Illustration XXVII-C. *The Nannie tucks the younger members of the family into bed in the nursery. The back of the room is marked with the easel and palette trademark and "Raphael Tuck & Sons Ltd., London, Paris and New York. Publishers to Their Majesties the King and Queen Alexandra. Printed in Germany." Size 2in high, 4in wide and 1¾in deep (6cm x 10cm x 4cm).*

LEFT: Color Illustration XXVIII. *"Sunny Susan" and her four costumes and matching hats from the "Little Maids New Series of Dressing Dolls." All are marked: "Raphael Tuck & Sons Ltd., London, Paris, Berlin, New York, Montreal. Published by Appointment to Their Majesties the King and Queen Alexandra." All pieces are marked with the Tuck trademark and the patent date of Feb. 20, 1894. Doll measures 13in (33cm).* Maurine Popp Collection.

ABOVE RIGHT: Color Illustration XXIX. *"Serene Sybil" with her four costumes and matching hats from the "Little Maids New Series of Dressing Dolls." All are marked with the Tuck trademark and "Published by Appointment to Their Majesties the King and Queen Alexandra. Patd. Feb. 20th 1894. Raphael Tuck & Sons Ltd., London, Paris, New York. Designed at the Studios in England and Printed at the Fine Art Works in Saxony." Doll measures 13in (33cm).* Maurine Popp Collection.

Color Illustrations XXX-A, B and C. "Playful Polly" and her four costumes and four hats. All are marked with the Tuck trademark and the patent date of Feb. 20, 1894. They are also marked: "Publishers by Appointment to Their Majesties the King and Queen Alexandra. Raphael Tuck & Sons Ltd., London, Paris, Berlin, New York, Montreal. Designed at the Studios in New York and Printed at the Fine Art Works in Saxony." Doll measures 13in (33cm). Maurine Popp Collection.

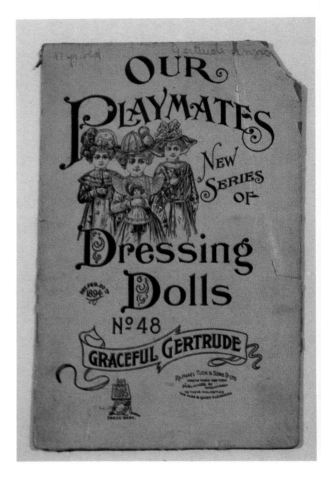

ABOVE: Color Illustration XXXII.
"Joyous Jessie" of "Our Playmates New Series of Dressing Dolls, No. 46." She and her costumes are marked with the easel and palette trademark, "Publishers by Appointment to Their Majesties the King and Queen Alexandra. Patd. Feb. 20th 1894. Raphael Tuck & Sons Ltd. London, Paris, New York. Designed at the Studios in England and Printed at the Fine Art Works in Saxony." Neither the doll or her costumes are numbered or named. Doll measures 9in (23cm). Maurine Popp Collection.

RIGHT: Color Illustration XXXI. "Fair Frances" with her four costumes from the "Little Maids New Series of Dressing Dolls." All are marked: "Raphael Tuck & Sons Ltd., London, Paris, New York. Publishers by Appointment to Their Majesties the King and Queen Alexandra. Designed at the Studios in New York and Printed at the Fine Art Works in Saxony." Doll measures 13in (33cm). Maurine Popp Collection.

Color Illustration XXXIII-A. The box cover for "Our Playmates New Series of Dressing Dolls, No. 48" and the doll "Graceful Gertrude." Both are marked with the easel and palette trademark and "Published by Appointment to Their Majesties the King and Queen Alexandra. Raphael Tuck & Sons Co., Ltd., London, Paris, New York." Box cover measures 10in x 6in (26cm x 15cm). Doll measures 9¾in (24cm). Maurine Popp Collection.

ABOVE: Color Illustration XXXIII-B. The four costumes and three hats for Graceful Gertrude. All pieces are marked with the easel and palette trademark and "Raphael Tuck & Sons Ltd., London, Paris, New York, Publishers by Appointment to Their Majesties the King and Queen Alexandra. Pat'd Feb. 20th, 1894. Designed at the Studios in England and Printed at the Fine Art Works in Saxony." Maurine Popp Collection.

Color Illustration XXXIV. *"Lovely Lilly" is No. 5 of "Dainty Dollies Series of Dressing Dolls" and is pictured with her original box cover and her costumes. She is marked the same as the cover with the addition of "Designed at the Studios in England and Printed at the Fine Art Works in Bavaria." Her costumes are marked as follows: Top row on the right of the doll is "Gown A." Bottom row, left to right is "Gown B," "Gown C" and "Gown D." Cover measures 9½in x 5½in (25cm x 14cm). Doll measures 9in (23cm). Jan Banneck Collection.*

Color Illustration XXXV. *"Fair Frances" is No. 8 of "Dainty Dollies Series of Dressing Dolls" and is pictured with the original box cover and her costumes. She is marked the same as the cover with the addition of "Designed at the Studios in England and Printed at the Fine Art Works in Bavaria." Her costumes are marked as follows: Top row, left to right is "Gown A" and "Gown B." The bottom row is "Gown C" and "Gown D." Cover measures 9½in x 5½in (25cm x 14cm). Doll measures 9in (23cm). Peggy Jo Rosamond Collection.*

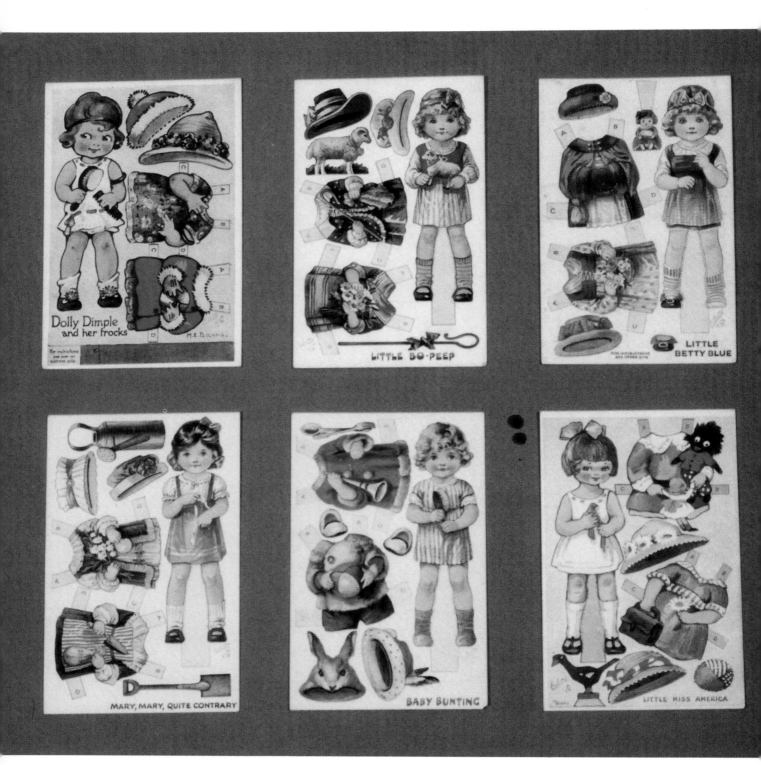

Color Illustration XXXVI. *Six "Pastime Postcards" picturing paper dolls to be cut out. The back of each card has printed instructions as to how to cut out and assemble these paper dolls. It also has the following information: Title and series number and the Tuck trademark, also "Raphael Tuck & Sons Oilette Postcard, Art Publishers to Their Majesties the King and Queen. Printed in England, Copyright London" and the artist's name. Cards measure 5½in x 3½in (14cm x 9cm) each. Jan Banneck Collection.*

in a bow at the neck. Her gloves are beige and she carries a bouquet of daisies in her right hand and carries a basket of fruit in her left. Her high laced boots are brown. The third costume is a pale blue party dress with a yellow and gold brocade evening coat trimmed with white fur. Her gloves are white and she carries a blue evening bag that matches the dress. The fourth costume is a long pink gown with lace-trimmed collar and cuffs. She holds a small kitten in her arms. Corresponding hats for each costume are shown. **(Illustration 128.)**

The second unmarked doll that we feel is one from the "Little Darlings" series is a pretty blonde with short, curly hair and a green bow on the left side of her hair. She is wearing a white chemise top laced with blue ribbon and a short blue petticoat. Her stockings and shoes are a reddish brown. The costumes, from left to right are as follows: A lovely party dress of soft green-gold with green stones. Her gloves, pocketbook and stockings are green and she carries a bouquet of red roses. Next is a dark blue coat with brown buttons and brown fur muff and collar. Her leggings are brown and buttoned on the side. Costume number three is a green tunic with a green and white striped blouse. The bow at her neck is lavender and she carries a slate and her school books. The fourth costume is a rose-colored party dress with white polka dots. Her gloves are white and she has a soft green scarf around her shoulders. She also has a bouquet of violets and an umbrella. Her stockings are pink and her shoes brown with pink bows. **(Illustration 129.)**

The "Our Playmates New Series of Dressing Dolls" do not have identification as to number or series name, but have the usual marking using the easel and palette trademark, "Publishers by Appointment to Their Majesties the King and Queen Alexanders. Patd. Feb. 20th 1894. Raphael Tuck & Sons Ltd., London, Paris, (note that Berlin has been dropped) New York. Designed at the Studios in England and printed at the Fine Art Works in Saxony."

"Joyous Jessie" is from the "Our Playmates New Series of Dressing Dolls." She is a blonde-haired paper doll with a blue ribbon in her hair. She is wearing a white chemise with rose-colored trim. Her four costumes and head pieces are coordinated as to style and color. Two of the costumes are accompanied by interesting doll items. **(Color Illustration XXXII.) Color Illustration XXXIII-A** pictures "Graceful Gertrude" and her original box cover from the "Our Playmates New Series of Dressing Dolls." **Color Illustration XXXIII-B** pictures the costumes belonging to Graceful Gertrude and this set is covered by the United States patent of Feb. 20th, 1894. **Color Illustration XXXIV** is "Lovely Lilly With Dresses and Hats." She is No. 5 of "Dainty Dollies Series of Dressing Dolls" and is pictured with her original box cover and her four dresses and three hats. She has dark blonde hair with a blue bow on the side. Her chemise and buttoned-on petticoat are white with blue ribbon trim. She has four costumes. Gown No. 5 A is a pale blue with lace trim and dark blue ribbon bows. Gown No. 5 B has a pale flowered pink underdress and a darker flowered pink overdress laced up in front. Gown No. 5 C is shades of tan and brown with braid trim in a soft blue-green. Gown No. 5 D is a light brown coat trimmed in red with a dark brown fur collar and muff. The hat is missing for this but is the one pictured on the cover.

Illustration 128. Another paper doll that is possibly from the "Little Darlings New Series of Dressing Dolls." The doll and her costumes are unmarked as to name and number but they all have the easel and palette trademark. All are also marked: "Publishers by Appointment to Their Majesties the King and Queen, Patd., Feb. 20th 1894. Raphael Tuck & Sons Ltd., London, Paris, Berlin, New York, Montreal. Designed at the Studios in New York and printed at the Fine Art Works in Saxony." Doll measures 13in (33cm). Maurine Popp Collection.

128-D.

128-A.

128-B.

128-C.

129-B.

129-C.

129-D.

129-A.

Illustration 129. *Possibly from the "Little Darlings New Series of Dressing Dolls." The doll and her costumes are unmarked as to name and number but do have the easel and palette trademark. All are also marked: "Publishers By Appointment to Their Majesties the King and Queen, Patd., Feb. 20th 1894. Raphael Tuck & Sons Ltd., London, Paris, Berlin, New York, Montreal. Designed at the Studios in New York and printed at the Fine Art Works in Saxony." Doll measures 13in (33cm). Maurine Popp Collection.*

Illustration 130 is "Gentle Gladys with Dresses and Hats." She is No. 6 of "Dainty Dollies Series of Dressing Dolls" and is pictured with four of her costumes. Two hats are missing. She has short blonde curly hair with a lavender bow on one side. Her two-piece undergarments are white and lavender. The chemise is white trimmed with lavender ribbon and the buttoned-on petticoat is lavender. Her four costumes are as follows: top left No. 6-D is a purple coat trimmed with ermine and she carries an ermine muff. On the right is No. 6-C, a green dress with wide white braid trim. She carries a red balloon. The lower left is Gown No. 6-A, a white gown with a yellow print design and trimmed with yellow ribbon and a red rose. Gown No. 6-B is a soft golden yellow with yellow ribbon trim. The wide bertha-style collar is lace.

Illustration 131 is "Sweet Sybel with Dresses and Hats." She is No. 7 of "Dainty Dollies Series of Dressing Dolls." She is pictured with her original box cover and her four costumes. Her hair is blonde and she has a light green ribbon on one side. The chemise is white, trimmed with green ribbon and the buttoned-on petticoat is soft green. Her four costumes are as follows: to the right of Sweet Sybel is a soft green party dress No. 7-A with lace trim around the collar and hips. She has a flowing green scarf held up by a bouquet of violets at the neck. She also holds a bouquet of violets in her left hand. The lower row from left to right is No. 7-B, a white dress with blue print and trimmed with blue ribbon. She holds a doll in her right hand. No. 7-C is a brown dress with gold ribbon trim. She holds a yellow chrysanthemum in her left hand. No. 7-D is a purple coat with chinchilla trim and muff. **Color Illustration XXXV** is "Fair Frances with Dresses and Hats." She is No. 8 of "Dainty Dollies Series of Dressing Dolls" and is pictured with her original box cover and her four costumes and hats. Her hair is dark brown and she is wearing a white chemise with pink trim. The petticoat is pink. The top row, from left to right, shows Gown No. 8-A, a yellow dress with white polka dots. Gown No. 8-B is white with a pink design and trimming. The lower row, from left to right, shows No. 8-C, a blue dress with white lace trim. No. 8-D is a red coat trimmed with white lace. The brown fur scarf matches the muff.

The following paper dolls are in the form of postcards and they are all within the 3300 and 3400 series and are commonly known as "Pastime Postcards." **Color Illustration XXXVI** pictures six examples that fall within this category. Each card has a doll with two costumes and hats and in some cases an accessory or a toy. The back of the card has the usual space on the right half for the address. On the left half is the printed directions for cutting and assembling. The tabs are marked: "A," "B," "C" and so on. Some of the cards have either a four or six-line verse below the instructions. This leaves very little room for a message and the sender's name if it is to be mailed. The left margin of the back of the card is marked with the title and number of the series as well as the seal of the royal coat-of-arms and the Tuck trademark. These cards are marked: "Raphael Tuck & Sons, Ltd., Art Publishers to Their Majesties the King and Queen, London, Paris and New York." This marking would put them in the 1901 to 1910 period, yet the cards illustrate children in the dress of the 1920 to 1930 period. This may indicate that the postcards carried the same marking into the 1930s. The Tuck markings seemed to be very accurate up to World War I on the paper dolls and toys. Most of the children's picture books did not always carry the monarch's reign and these postcard markings are a bit confusing. This bit of confusion is also evident in some of the paper dolls and toys published after World War I. The six postcards pictured are titled, from left to right, the top row is "Dolly Dimple and Her Frocks," "Little Bo-Peep" and "Little Betty Blue" and on the bottom row is "Mary, Mary, Quite Contrary," "Baby Bunting" and "Little Miss America."

The following is a listing of Raphael Tuck & Sons paper doll "Pastime Postcards."

Postcard No. 3381. "Dressing Doll Series I," signed "M. Banks."
1. "Dolly Dimple and Her Frocks." A British girl holding a comb and brush (**Color Illustration XXXVI**).
2. "Our Jimmy." A British boy, a suit with a flag and a suit with a puppy.
3. "Tommy Lad." A Scottish boy.
4. "Pretty Peggy and Her Frocks." A British girl with a coat, hat, apron and apples.
5. "Jack At Play." A British boy with nautical clothing.
6. "Little Pamela and Her Frocks." One clown dress and hat. She holds a doll in her arms with her second outfit.

Postcard No. 3382. "Nursery Rhymes Dressing Dolls, Series II," signed "M. Banks."
1. "Baby Bunting." (**Color Illustration XXXVI**).
2. "The Knave of Hearts."
3. "Little Miss Muffet."
4. "Little Bo Peep." (**Color Illustration XXXVI**).
5. "Little Jack Horner."
6. "Mary, Mary, Quite Contrary." (**Color Illustration XXXVI**).

Postcard No. 3383. "Nursery Rhymes Dressing Dolls Series III."
1. "Little Betty Blue." (**Color Illustration XXXVI**).
2. "Little Boy Blue."
3. "Handy, Spandy JackOaDandy."
4. "Simple Simon."
5. "The Queen of Hearts."
6. "Tom, Tom the Piper's Son."

Postcard No. 3384. "Dressing Dolls, Series," signed "M. Banks."
1. "Little Miss America." (**Color Illustration XXXVI**).
2. "Little Miss America."
3. "Little Miss Spain."
4. "A Little Bit of China."
5. "The Little Dutch Girl."
6. "Vive La France."

Illustration 132 pictures the front and back of the tan envelope that packages six postcards within a series. On the face of the envelope is a line drawing of a paper doll of Postcard No. 3383, "Dressing Dolls, Series III." It is also marked: "A novel and charming Series of Six different Dolls with two changes of dresses and hats

Illustration 130. "Gentle Gladys" of the "Dainty Dollies Series of Dressing Dolls." She is marked with her name and "No. 6." The easel and palette trademark is also seen, plus "Publishers to Their Majesties the King and Queen. Raphael Tuck & Sons Ltd. London, Paris, Berlin, New York and Montreal. Designed at the Studios in England, and Printed at the Fine Art Works in Bavaria." The costumes are numbered. Top row, left to right, No. 6 D, No. 6 C and on the lower left No. 6 A and No. 6 B. Doll measures 9in (23cm). Joyce Alexander Collection.

6-D.

6-A.

6-B.

6-C.

137

Illustration 131. This original cover is marked: "Sweet Sybel with Dresses and Hats, No. 7" of "Dainty Dollies Series of Dressing Dolls." The easel and palette trademark, "Raphael Tuck & Sons Co. Ltd. Publishers to Their Majesties the King and Queen. London, Paris, Berlin, New York, Montreal." The doll is marked with her name and in addition to the markings on the cover, "Designed at the Studios in England and Printed at the Fine Art Works in Bavaria." The costumes are numbered. Top row, right, No. 7 A; lower row, left to right, No. 7 B, No. 7 C and No. 7 D. Cover measures 9½in x 5¼in (25cm x 14cm). Doll measures 9in (23cm). Joyce Alexander Collection.

Illustration 132. The front and back of the tan envelope that packages six postcards within a series. This is from "Dressing Dolls, Series III." Envelope measures 6in x 4in (15cm x 10cm). Jan Banneck Collection.

made to cut out and stand up, affording endless amusement and delight to young folk." The back of the envelope carries much information regarding the different types of Tuck printed postcards. Such series as "Oilette," "Oilfacsim," "Carbonette," "Gravure" and "Water Colour" are mentioned. It also mentions "Tuck's Postcard Exchange Register, the twentieth yearly issue, which contains the names of upwards of 2000 ladies and gentlemen collectors of Tuck postcards in every part of the world, who will exchange Tuck postcards with you." The sales pitch ends with the wording: "Tuck's Postcard Exchange Register, incorporated with Tuck's Postcard List will be sent post free on application to Raphael Tuck & Sons, Ltd., Publishers to Their Majesties the King and Queen, Raphael House, Moorfield City, London."

Chapter III

Part I
The Reign of King George V and Queen Mary, 1910-1936
Production Before and After World War I

We approach a new era in 1910 as King Edward passes on and the Prince and Princess of Wales become George V and Queen Mary. Alexandra became the Queen Mother. The names of these three royal personalities appear on all the Tuck products from 1910 until 1925 when Queen Alexandra died. This chapter will cover the entire period from 1910 to 1936 that George V ruled.

During this period, the Tuck company continued with its energetic publishing program. This included puzzles, postcards, Christmas cards, holiday cards and several new series of children's books. **(Illustration 133.)** In 1913, Desmond Tuck visited the United States for the sole purpose of introducing the idea of personalized Christmas cards on which the name of the sender would be printed. American wholesalers rejected the idea, feeling that customers preferred to sign their own cards. It was in this same year that the Tuck firm closed its Montreal branch which had opened in 1907.

As World War I appeared on the scene, Reginald Tuck went into Army service. His brother, Desmond, volunteered for overseas service, spending time with the French Air Force, then with the Royal Flying Corps and ultimately with the Royal Air Force. The firm of Raphael Tuck & Sons was affected in other ways as a result of the start of the war. A notice concerning the firm appeared in two trade publications, the *Worlds Paper Trade Review* published in London and *Toys and Novelties* published in the United States. The notice appearing in the June 1915 issue of the American trade magazine stated, "Tuck's Berlin Business Sequestrated By The Germans." The article read as follows: "Messrs. Raphael Tuck & Sons have been notified by the board of trade that an announcement has appeared in the Reichsanjeiger, the official gazette of the German Empire, that the branch business established by the firm in Berlin in 1907, for the sale of their Oilette postcard and other British publications has been seized, and the business and assets sold by the German authorities." "It appears that soon after the outbreak of the war this Berlin branch of Raphael Tuck & Sons, which was in a most profitable state, important sums being due the company at the time from customers throughout Germany and Austria, was taken over by the German government. Shortly afterwards violent attacks directed against Messrs Raphael Tuck & Sons appeared in a leading Berlin journal, calling upon the German public to boycott the production of the well known British house. Similar articles were published in some 200 journals throughout the German Empire. These attacks finally culminating in the sequestration of the business by the authorities."

Raphael Tuck & Sons, in their reply to this official information, intimated to the Board of Trade that they would naturally look for the intervention of His Majesty's government with regard to the takeover of their property at the conclusion of the war.

At the end of hostilities, both Reginald and Desmond returned to the family business. The company soon caught up to its pre-war level. Desmond realized the

Illustration 133. A full-page advertisement that appeared in an 1910 issue of the American toy trade publication Playthings. *It pictures a group of humorous Halloween postcards and a selection of Thanksgiving postcards. Notice the wholesale price of $1.00 per gross. Page size 10in x 7½in (25cm x 19cm).*

ultimate result of his earlier pre-war visit to the United States. The American wholesalers had rethought the idea of personalized Christmas cards and found that they would sell with considerable success. It was in the following decade in growth of Raphael Tuck & Sons Ltd., that the firm saw not only new publishing developments, but a number of important contributions by Reginald and Desmond Tuck.

While we have not as yet mentioned storybooks offered during this reign, Tuck continued to publish several series. One very interesting example is titled *More About The Three Bears* from "Father Tuck's Little Pets Series." This story is a sequel to *Goldilocks and the Three Bears*. In general, the story goes as follows: About a week after Goldilocks had jumped out the window of the bear's house and escaped, the Little Bear came down for breakfast one morning. And surprise, there sitting in Mother Bear's lap were two tiny bears, twins. **Illustration 134** pictures the front cover of the new book, showing the original family, and the back cover picturing the twins at one year of age. The story continues on to tell about the growth of the twins and how the family adapted to them.

During the late 1880s, Tuck published many decorative and unusual valentines. They published a number of larger showy stand-up types. These novelties, which folded flat for mailing, could be opened up and made to stand upright. They represented carriages, trains, ships and other types of whimsical subjects colorfully decorated with the usual hearts and cupid ornamentation. They also produced a wide variety of designs and verses — on postcard-type valentines.

Interest in valentines after the World War I dwindled in Great Britain. The year 1925 was the Diamond Jubilee of the founding of the Tuck company and Lady Jeanetta Tuck suggested to her husband, Adolph, that the company should try to revive the public's interest in valentines. Adolph agreed and in 1926, the firm published a large assortment of valentines and earnestly engaged in their promotion. The fancy, possibly over-done lacy decoration of the pre 1900 card was more or less gone. The large and beautiful mechanicals of the 1900-1910 period disappeared, while the shapely ladies in their early costumes gave way to thinner ladies in shorter new-style dresses of the later 1920s. **(Illustration 135.)** As time passes, people's ideas change, dress changes, designs of valentines change, while affairs of the heart stay more or less the same. **(Illustrations 136 & 137.)**

While the Tuck company continued its tremendous production of various types of postcards during this 1910-1936 period, mention should be made of those published picturing the various rooms that made up Titania's Palace. While this wonderful palace is not a paper toy, it was an edifice of imagination for both adults and children. Here was a home for the Good Fairies and their queen, Titania. Fairyland has always occupied a part of a child's imagination, hopefully influencing thought and action. Fairies suggest to every child that a good thought leads to a good and useful deed. This was Titania's secret; help those who are neglected and unhappy.

Sir Nevile Wilkinson was the creator and architect of Titania's Palace. The floor plan of the palace was in the form of a hollow rectangle, 9ft x 7ft (2.7m x 2.1m),

Illustration 134. The back and front covers of a book titled More About The Three Bears *from Father Tuck's "Little Pet Series," No. 8340. The book is marked with the easel and palette trademark and "Raphael Tuck & Sons, Ltd., London-Paris-New York-Berlin-Montreal, Publishers to Their Majesties the King & Queen and Her Majesty Queen Alexandra, Designed at the Studios in England and Printed at the Fine Art Works in Germany." Book size is 9in high and 7½in wide (23cm x 18cm).*

Illustration 135. Three cute valentine children equipped with movable bonnets that move to cover up or reveal their smiling faces. Colors are soft pink, red and blue; they are very appealing. Each is equipped with a rear folding stand. Each is marked: "Raphael Tuck & Sons, Ltd., London, Paris, Berlin, New York, Montreal" and the trademark. Figure stands 6in high (15cm). Grayce Piemontesi Collection.

occupying an area of 63 square feet. The total height is 27in (69cm) and it was built in sections so that it could be dismantled and packed for travel. **(Illustration 138.)** Sir Nevile furnished and decorated the 16-room palace with his extensive collection of miniatures, many of which were antiques. Many others were crafted and painted by Wilkinson.

Titania's Palace was opened by Queen Mary on July 6, 1922, at an exhibition open to the public at the Women's Exhibition at Olympia. Since that time, it has visited more than 150 cities in Great Britain, the United States, South America, Australia and New Zealand. It has been viewed and appreciated by millions of people and has raised tens of thousands of pounds for the welfare of crippled, neglected and unhappy children.

When Queen Mary opened the exhibition featuring Titania's Palace, Raphael Tuck & Sons Ltd., published an extensive line of postcards featuring the palace and its lavishly furnished interior. **(Illustrations 139-A & 139-B.)** Many editions of these cards were published over the years as the palace traveled from country to country. Titania's Palace came to its present resting place in Tivoli Gardens in Denmark in the early 1980s. This Palace of the Fairies is still viewed by thousands of believers, both young and old.

The Tuck company's earlier venture of the publishing of Sir Nevile Wilkinson's "Titania's Palace" postcards was followed by the issuing of a still more extensive series of cards, those portraying the "Queen's Dolls' House".

Possibly the most intriguing and unusual group of sets of postcards published by Raphael Tuck & Sons was those picturing the interior rooms of the Queen's Dolls' House. This outstanding beautiful doll house was presented to Queen Mary in 1924. Over 1600 craftsmen and artists outdid themselves to create this sensational model. The doll house measured 8ft (2.4m) high by 5ft (1.5m) high and contained 30 rooms including bathrooms and closets. The scale was 1in (3cm) to 1ft (31cm). **(Illustration 140.)** After the presentation to Queen Mary, the dolls' house was placed in exhibition at Windsor Castle and later in various cities of

Illustration 136. Two novelty-type valentines from the 1920s that feature applied eyes. The little girl has large bead-like blue eyes while the boy has floating eyes that move when the card is shaken. Both cards have a valentine message inside and are hinged at the top so that they will stand. Each is marked with the easel and palette trademark and "Raphael Tuck & Sons Ltd., London, Paris, New York." The little girl stands 8in (20cm) tall. Grayce Piemontesi Collection.

Britain and also traveled extensively overseas. Proceeds from the traveling exhibits helped to benefit the Queen's charities. At the start of these exhibits, the Queen's Dolls' House Committee contacted the firm of Raphael Tuck & Sons to see if they would be interested in publishing postcards showing the dolls' house, the interior rooms and their miniature contents.

The Tuck firm honored the request by producing six sets of eight postcards each. Today, the ownership of the six complete sets along with their original envelopes is the dream of postcard and/or miniature collectors. The following is a description of the dolls' house card series plus descriptive information gathered from *The Book of The Queen's Dolls' House* edited by A. C. Benson, C.V.O. and Sir Lawrence Weaver, K.B.C.

Set No. I pictures views of the Garden Entrance, the Entrance Hall, then a close-up of the Hall Table and Chairs, the Dining Table, the Dining Room Fireplace, the Dining Room Sideboard, the China Coffee Service and lastly, a view of the Wine Cellar.

A more detailed description of the above cards follows; The Garden Entrance view pictures the wonderful wrought iron gates, the tall evergreens, the formal clipped hedges and flower gardens. **(Illustration 140.)** The next card is a photograph taken from the door of the Entrance Hall. It shows the magnificent sweeping marble stairway with its decorative wrought iron balustrade. The white marble floor emphasizes the colorful wall mural by William Nicholson which depicts the expulsion of Adam and Eve from the Garden of Eden. A hall table holds a guest book and an ink stand. A statue of Venus and suits of armor complete the contents of the card. **(Illustration 141-A.)**

Card number three pictures the Dining Room. It has a decorated ceiling, a figured rug and portraits of the Royal Family and others are hung on the ivory and gold walls. The next card shows the dining room table covered with white linen and fully set with china, silver, candelabra, fruit and flowers. The next card shows the sienna and white marble fireplace that has a mantelpiece that holds two Sevres vases, two silver cups and a clock that actually tells time. The next card pictures the sideboard with its silver servers, rosewater bowls and some racing trophies. The final card of this first series pictures the Wine Cellar. It contains many varieties of real wine; each bottle sports a miniature label of a famous wine maker. Wine cases are piled on the floor and a carrying basket is placed to one side. **(Illustration 141-C.)**

Set number two pictures views of the grand piano in the Drawing Room **(Illustration 141-D)**, the Drawing Room cabinet, other Drawing Room furniture, the Library, some of the Library furniture, the King's library table, a corner of the Library and the regalia in the Strong Room. Card number one in this set pictures the grand piano, built on a scale of an 1in (3cm) to 1ft (31cm); it can be played. The

ABOVE: Illustration 137. Two highly-colored and embossed die-cut valentines. On the top a boy and girl are dancing and on the bottom is a comical boy with revolving features. The dancing pair are printed on both sides and are folded at the clasped hands which enables them to stand on their toes. They stand 5¼in (13cm) high. The comic boy stands 6½in (17cm). He is marked with the easel and palette trademark and "Raphael Tuck & Sons Ltd., Publishers to Their Majesties the King and Queen."

Illustration 138. The north facade of "Titania's Palace," a magnificent 16-room palace where fairies dwell. The card is marked: "Titania's Palace, Series 1, Raphael Tuck & Sons Oilette Postcard No. 4521, Art Publishers to Their Majesties the King & Queen, Copyright London, Printed in England." Card size 3½in x 5½in (9cm x 14cm).

Illustration 139-A. *The "Hall of the Fairy Kiss." The staircase leads to the Minstrel Gallery; a portrait of H. M. Queen Alexandra is positioned on the wall at the top of the staircase. Markings on the back of the card and its size are similar to that of* Illustration 138.

Illustration 139-B. *The "Great Throne Room of Fairyland," 27in (69cm) high. Note the famous mosaic frieze. On the left is the bronze fairy and above her and the throne is a fine group of infant Bacchanals in Sevres biscuit china. Markings on the back of the card are similar to those on the two previous cards.*

Drawing Room cabinet is a model of one owned by the Marquis of Londonderry. Its tiny pull-out drawers may all be locked with a small gold key. A third Drawing Room view shows a table on which is placed a Raphael Tuck calender, a Louis XV settee and a tapestry upholstered chair. The next card provides a view of the Library with its walls lined with bookcases which contain some 200 leather bound volumes by famous authors. **(Illustration 141-E.)** Another card pictures a large walnut table on which stands the King's dispatch boxes. Its drawers contain 750 miniature watercolors, drawings and etchings contributed by noted artists. A further card pictures the King's library table which holds pens, a paperweight, a cheque book and various desk ornaments. The final card in this series is that showing the Strong Room. Behind steel bars are the King's and Queen's crowns and other Royal Jewels, all set with real jewels.

Set number three provides views of the Royal sleeping quarters, the King's Bedroom, his Bathroom, the Queen's Bedroom, the Queen's Bathroom, the Queen's Bed, the Wardrobe and Chest of Drawers in the Queen's Room, views of other furniture and the Princess Royal's Room.

The King's Bedroom has a painted ceiling, special woven rugs and wall hangings. **(Illustration 141-F.)** His bathroom is of green marble while the wash basin and tub is equipped with taps that actually provide running water. The walls are decorated with Punch cartoons. Another card pictures the Queen's Bathroom in shagreen and ivory, an ornamental tub and a chest on which is placed a Faberge Japanese tree set with diamonds.

The next card shows the Queen's bed hung with woven blue and silver damask while the bedspread is embroidered with seed pearls. **(Illustration 141-G.)** The final card displays the Princess Royal's Room in which the furnishings are very plain.

Set number four contains views of the Queen's Boudoir, a gold tea and coffee service, the carpet in the Queen's Bedroom, a Chinese cabinet, the fireplace and mantel in the Queen's Bedroom, her writing desk and chair, her dressing table and the Linen Room.

The walls of the Queen's Boudoir are covered with brown silk on which is a lotus flower design painted by Edmund Dulac. The chairs are bamboo Chippendale while the ornaments and vases are of Chinese jade. **(Illustration 141-H.)** The next card pictures a close-up of the tiny gold tea service. The third card pictures a lovely carpet in soft pastel shades, woven at the Weaving School for Crippled Girls. The decorative fireplace, made of white marble inlaid with jade, is an object of unusual beauty. Above it is a miniature painting of the Queen Mother. A further card shows the Queen's dressing table, with a glass top covered with such objects as a trinket or jewel box, powder boxes, perfume bottles, and so forth. The final card features the Linen Room with a miniature sewing machine that works and shelves of stacked linen, all bearing the Royal monogram.

Set number five shows views of the Royal Nursery, the cradle, a baby chair and weighing scales. The Nursery piano and gramophone, a china tea and toilet set, a

Illustration 140. *An end view of the "Garden Entrance" of "The Queen's Dolls' House," a beautiful garden with its elaborate entrance gates. Back of card is marked: "The Queen's Dolls House, Series 1, Raphael Tuck & Sons Oilette Postcard No. 4500, Art Publishers to Their Majesties The King & Queen, Copyright London, Printed in England." Card size 5½in x 3½in (14cm x 9cm).*

Illustration 141-A. *The "Entrance Hall" of the "Queen's Dolls' House." Note the curved sweep of the white marble stairs and the lapis lazuli and white marble checkered floor. This later edition postcard carries the markings: "The Queen's Dolls' House, Series BC, Raphael Tuck & Sons Ltd., By Appointment to Her Majesty the Queen, Fine art Publishers." Card size 4⅛in x 5⅞in (11cm x 15cm).*

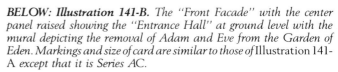

BELOW: *Illustration 141-B. The "Front Facade" with the center panel raised showing the "Entrance Hall" at ground level with the mural depicting the removal of Adam and Eve from the Garden of Eden. Markings and size of card are similar to those of Illustration 141-A except that it is Series AC.*

Illustration 141-C. *"The Wine Cellar" with its 1in (3cm) to 1ft (31cm) scale bottles, boxes and casks. Markings and size of card are identical to those mentioned for the previous card.*

Illustration 141-D. *"The Drawing Room" or "Grand Saloon" with its miniature portraits of British rulers. Markings and size of card are identical to the one before it.*

group of nursery toys and Father Tuck's Annual, the Housemaids Closet, the Royal Kitchen and the kitchen table.

The Royal Nursery is simple and rather plain, yet nothing is lacking in the way of comfort or entertainment. The walls are decorated with illustrations of characters from juvenile fairy tales. Playthings such as a toy theater, a rocking horse, a Noah's Ark, a train and other toys that would keep any child contented are included. (**Illustration 141-I.**) The second card displays the Royal Nursery cradle. It is constructed of apple wood with ivory decorations. It features the Prince of Wales' crested feathers on the hood and a guardian angel kneeling at the foot. The weighing scale actually works. The piano is ivory color and its rack holds miniature song sheets, while the tiny gramophone plays a tiny record of "God Save the King." A further card features the tea service and toilet set, both made in Stoke-on-Trent, home of English Art Pottery. The next card pictures the Royal Kitchen which contains a range and ovens equipped with sliding trays and movable doors. The shelves hold miniature Doulton jars of flour, salt, sugar, and so forth, and pots and pans. The card picturing the kitchen table has everything needed by a cook of a royal household, objects such as molds and pans, a mincing machine and a coffee mill. (**Illustration 141-J.**) The final postcard in this series pictures the Household Closet. It has a sink with running water and a teak drain board; both are backed by Dutch tiles. Other cleaning equipment such as brooms, mops, pails, brushes, soaps and polishes are present along with a vacuum cleaner and step ladder.

Set number six is titled "Round About the House." It features postcards illustrating the House and Garden, the Garage, a Perambulator and Motorcycle, Croquet Set and other sporting equipment. Outdoor equipment, the Storehouse in the Cellar, the Electric Lighting and Water System and lastly the Fire Escape. As mentioned earlier, the Queen's Dolls' House measures 8ft (2.4m) long and 5ft (1.5m) high. The second card pictures a view of the garage with its miniature automobiles. (**Illustration 141-K.**) A third card pictures a motorcycle with a side car and an elaborate perambulator carrying the Royal Emblem. The sport equipment is all built to a scale of 1in to 1ft (31cm). One card illustrates the Cellar Storerooms, which are correctly labeled. The water system in this miniature house is supplied from a cistern on the roof and piped to the various taps within the interior. The lighting fixtures are operated by electricity as are the tiny elevators which run up and down to the various levels. The last card pictures the Fire Escape and some of the fire fighting equipment.

This has been rather a long and fairly detailed description of the six sets of postcards pertaining to the Queen's Dolls' House. But Raphael Tuck & Sons did a wonderful job in picturing these miniature objects on postcards and happy is the collector who finds them.

Sorrow struck the British Empire in 1925 when Her Majesty Queen Alexandra passed away. A year later in July, Sir Adolph Tuck was laid to rest. The Tuck company's revival of the valentines and the publishing of the series of Titania's Palace postcards and those of the Queen's Dolls' House were the last important venture of Sir Adolph Tuck's many growth enterprises. His eldest son, Reginald, succeeded to his title. Gustave Tuck became Chairman and Managing Director of the company, Sir Reginald and his brother, Desmond, continued on the board.

ABOVE LEFT: Illustration 141-E. This "Library" contains some 200 leather bound volumes containing the works of famous authors. The back of the card is marked: "The Queen's Dolls House, Series II, Raphael Tuck & Sons Oilette Postcard No. 4501, Art Publishers to Their Majesties the King & Queen, Copyright London, Printed in England." Size 3⅞in x 5⅜in (9cm x 14cm).

ABOVE RIGHT: Illustration 141-F. "The King's Bedroom" pictures his bed hung with specially woven silk. The miniature portrait over the fireplace is that of Princess Mary. Markings on card and size are identical to the previous card except that it is part of Series III and is No. 4502.

Illustration 141-G. *"The Queen's Bedroom" is decorated in a soft blue-gray accented with white. The ceiling is painted to represent the sky with small cherubs flying about the clouds. Card size and markings are identical to that in Illustration 141-F.*

Illustration 141-H. *"Her Majesty's Boudoir" walls are painted silk, the bamboo chairs Chippendale in style and the rug is an exact reproduction in miniature of a Chinese carpet of the Chien Lung period. Card size and markings are identical to the card in Illustration 141-G, except it is marked: "Series IV" and "No. 4503."*

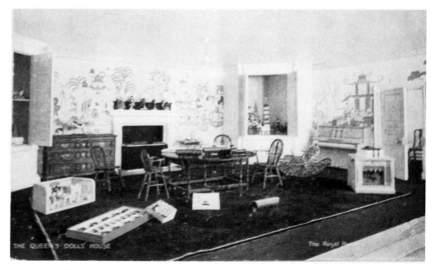

ABOVE: Illustration 141-I. *"The Royal Nursery" walls were decorated by Edmund Dulac. They illustrate famous fairy tales. The room contains a number of playthings that were popular in the 1920s, all in miniature. Card size and markings are similar to the two preceding cards except it is marked: "Series V" and "No. 4504."*

ABOVE: Illustration 141-K. *The opposite side of the house which was the "Garden Entrance." This shows the garage with its six limousines, the library and the King's Bedroom above it. This card has the same markings and size as the card in Illustration 141-J.*

RIGHT: Illustration 141-J. *"The Royal Kitchen" with its parquet floor and tiled walls, a series of built-in ovens and stove and all the equipment needed to complete a modern kitchen of the 1920s. Markings on this card are identical to the one before it.*

Chapter III

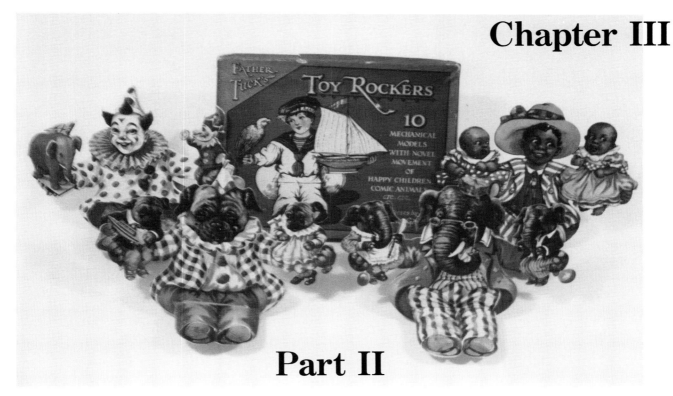

Part II

The Reign of King George V and Queen Mary, 1910-1936
Paper Toys Before and After World War I

Raphael Tuck & Sons Ltd., published a number of intriguing paper toys before and after World War I. A fine example of such a toy published before the war was "Father Tuck's Toy Rockers," a boxed set consisting of ten mechanical models. **Illustration 142** pictures four of the ten toys and the box cover. In the forefront are "Puppy Pugs" and "Jumbo and His Babies." The second row features "The Merry Clown" on the left and "A Bright Darkie" on the right with the box cover pictured center rear. The other six toys are titled "Lovely Louise," "A Well-known Friend," "Red Riding Hood," "From China Town," "A Proud Parent" and "Toy Joy." The back of each toy is marked with its appropriate title and an accompanying four-line verse by Norman Gale. These rockers are unique in construction in that a second rocker is positioned on the back and that the figure's lower legs are connected to the back rocker and protrude through a horizontal slit above the front rocker, revealing the lower legs and feet of the subject represented. All figures are highly colored, glazed, die-cut and embossed.

Another pre-war example was titled "With Father Tuck At The Circus." **Illustration 143-A** pictures the colorful cover of the panorama. This large four-section panorama pictures four circus performances. Each section has four horizontal slits, each of which accepts the base tab supporting a clown, a performer or a circus animal. The first section contains two clowns, one of which is standing on a railing holding a hoop through which a lady bareback rider, standing on the backs of three galloping horses, will jump as she approaches the hoop and land back on the horses. A Ring Master with a whip stands in the center of the ring. The second section pictures a small elephant standing on his head, a big brown bear being led around by a small dog and a seated clown teaching a sitting pig the ABCs. **(Illustration 143-B.)** The third section features a clown riding a bucking donkey, another clown saluting a dog dressed as a soldier and lastly, a small terrier pushing a barrel on which a white poodle is balancing. The last section shows a black poodle sitting on the back of a trotting horse, a monkey dressed in racing colors riding a

Illustration 142. "Father Tuck's Toy Rockers" original box and four of the ten mechanical rocking models of happy children and comic animals. Box and figures are marked: "Raphael Tuck & Sons Ltd., London-Paris-Berlin-New York-Montreal." Figures have the additional markings: "Publishers by Appointment to Their Majesties The King and Queen and to Queen Alexandra, Designed in England and Printed in Saxony." Average size of rocking figures 6¼in high, 9½in wide and 4½in deep (17cm x 24cm x 11cm).

ABOVE: *Illustration 143-A. The cover of a large folding panorama titled "With Father Tuck At The Circus." The back cover is marked with assembling directions, the easel and palette trademark and "No. 7891," also "Raphael Tuck & Sons Ltd., London-Paris-Berlin-New York-Montreal, Publishers to Their Majesties The King & Queen and Her Majesty Queen Alexandra, Designed at the Studios in England and Printed at the Fine Art Works in Germany." Panorama measures 9⅞in high by 12½in wide (25cm x 32cm). Open, it extends to 50in (128cm).*

Illustration 143-B. The second section of a four-part panorama titled "With Father Tuck At The Circus." Each section is 9⅞in high by 12½in wide (25cm x 32cm).

pony, a Golliwog riding on a white poodle and a little dog dressed in a lady's shopping dress. **(Illustration 143-C.)** The backs of the two center sections carry a series of verses concerning the pictured performers of the circus. The verses are written by Clifton Bingham.

Tuck published a series of painting books during this period, some 37 in all. Listed as "Father Tuck's Patent Paintbox Series," they were far superior to those mentioned in earlier periods. There were large, colorful eight-page booklets with six oval holes along the top revealing color tabs attached to the inside back cover. **Illustration 144-A** pictures the *Dresses For Dolly Painting Book*. **Illustration 144-B** shows the first two pages of the book, the fully-colored illustrations on the left page to copy and the outlines on the right to be painted in. Instructions for little artists are printed on the inside back cover under the row of watercolor slips. Briefly, it mentions that all the little artist needs is a brush and a glass of water. Then the method of applying the watercolors and then how to cut and fold the paper dolls. The back cover of the book pictures five or six color illustrations of various booklet covers in the series and a listing of the titles available. In the corners are the markings: "German Patent 190062, United Kingdom Patent Nos. 11146 & 5207, French Patent No. 372263 and United States Patent, Jan. 15, 1907." **Illustration 145** pictures the back cover of one of the other Tuck painting books in the same series. Illustrated are six covers of painting books that cover a variety of subjects.

Raphael Tuck & Sons published a variety of postcards that could be cut out and made into toys. These die-cut punch outs or figures could be cut out and then assembled into a toy that would stand, rock or swing. These were known as "Tuck's Pastime Postcards" and were eagerly sought-after by children between 1920 through the 1930s. Unfortunately, this is why not too many intact examples of the Pastime postcards exist today. Many of these cards are classified as paper dolls and they will be covered later in the paper doll section. There are a number that can be mentioned and pictured here. The various titled series have a specific number; each series consists of six cards.

The first group is titled "The Fairy Land Panorama Series," No. 3386. All six cards are marked with the same information, except for the title on each card and a paragraph of instructions for assembling. This series consists of 1. "Beauty and the Beast" which pictures five die-cut characters: Beauty, the Beast, the Father, the Sister and the Maid. 2. "Cinderella" with the characters Cinderella, the Prince, the two Sisters and a Servant who carries the Glass Slipper **(Illustration 146)**, "Jack and the Beanstalk" with the characters of Jack, his mother, a cow, a hen and a harp. 4. "Little Snow White" has three punch-out characters, Snow White, the Queen and a grouping of seven Dwarfs. 5. "Red Riding Hood" with seven punch outs consisting of Little Red Riding Hood, the Wolf, the Grandmother, the Forester, a rabbit, a hare and a squirrel. 6. "Sleeping Beauty" with five characters consisting of Sleeping Beauty before and after, her parents, the King and Queen and the Wicked Fairy.

The second group, Postcard No. 3387, was the "Model Cottage, Series I." These were from original paintings by E. Heatly. They consisted of six British cottages to be cut out, scored, folded and tabs inserted into slots to produce a free-

Illustration 143-C. *The last section of the four-part panorama picturing four animal acts in "Father Tuck's Panorama Circus." This last section measures 9⅞in high by 12½in wide (25cm x 32cm).*

standing cottage. 1. Titled "Ye Olde Boar's Head." 2. A brown roofed cottage with diamond-shaped window panes. 3. A red roof cottage with small square windowpanes and a dog sitting at the rear door **(Illustration 147)**. 4. A girl sitting on a bench near the cottage door while a boy waves his hand in a window. 5. A child and her dog sit on the steps of a red roof cottage. 6. A girl stands by a window near the back door, a cat sits on the front steps.

The third group marked: "Postcard No. 3388, A Model Cottage, Series II" is similar in subject matter to the preceding group. All six cards make up small British cottages.

The fourth group is marked: "Postcards No. 3390, Butterflies on the Wing." Series I consists of foreign moths and butterflies, signed by an A. L. West. Series II displays British moths drawn by Weatly. Series III displays British moths by N. Brady. Series IV is a further group of moths by N. Brady.

The fifth group is marked: "Postcard No. 3394, Mechanical Dolls, Series I," signed by M. Banks. Each of the six cards has a pillow with the card title, a seated costumed figure, a head with a long tab to be inserted into the neck of the figure, a

ABOVE: Illustration 144-A. *The cover of the Dresses For Dolly Painting Book. The back cover is marked with the easel and palette trademark and "No. 4020," also "Raphael Tuck & Sons Ltd., London-Paris-Berlin-New York-Montreal, Publishers to Their Majesties The King & Queen and H.H. Queen Alexandra, Designed at the Studios in England, Printed in Bavaria." Size 10⅝in high by 7⅞in wide (27cm x 20cm).*

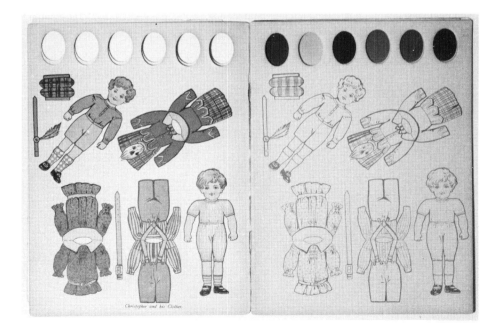

Illustration 144-B. *The first two pages of the painting book, the color illustration on the left to be copied and the line drawing on the right to be painted in. Size open 10⅝in x 15¾in (27cm x 40cm).*

149

Illustration 145. The back cover of one of the other painting books which is presented in horizontal form, although the information on it is similar to that found on the others in the series. Size 7⅞in high by 10⅝in wide (20cm x 27cm).

RIGHT: Illustration 146. "Cinderella," one of six postcards in a group titled "The Fairy Land Panorama Series, No. 3386." Back of card is marked: "Raphael Tuck & Sons Oilette, Art Publishers to Their Majesties the King & Queen, After the Original Painting by A. L. Bowley." Size 5½in x 3½in (14cm x 9cm). Jan Banneck Collection.

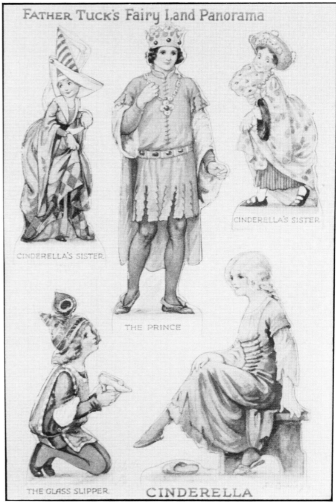

BELOW: Illustration 147. An "English Cottage," one of six postcards in a group called "Model Cottages, Series I., No. 3387." Marked: "After the original painting by E. Heatley." All other markings are similar to those on the back of the preceding "Cinderella" postcard. Size 3½in x 5½in (9cm x 14cm). Jan Banneck Collection.

hat and an accessory. When cut, folded and assembled, the completed figure sits upright on the pillow. The six cards are: 1. "A Bonnie Highland Laddie" which consists of a boy playing his bagpipes with a dog standing by. 2. "The Little Colleen," a girl with a basket of eggs and a pig. 3. "The Little Flower Girl," an Italian girl holding pots of flowers. 4. "A Little Welsh Maid," a little girl knitting. 5. "The Little Shepherds," a girl holds lamb and staff, a second lamb stands at her feet. 6. "Somebody's Sweetheart," a British girl holds a teddy bear while a doll sits at her side. **(Illustration 148.)**

The sixth group falls under "Postcard No. 3394, Mechanical Dolls, Series II." Each of the six cards has a title at the bottom of the card. Each pictures a headless figure in a foreign costume, a head with a long neck tab to be inserted into the neck of the figure. The accessories are to be cut out and inserted into slots on the figures' hands. When assembled, the figures will sit or stand upright. The following are the six titled cards with a brief description. 1. "A Bonnie Highland Laddie," a standing boy with bagpipes. He is accompanied by a dog and bears a sword and a tam. 2. "A Little Fortune Teller," a seated girl in a turban with a basket and apples. 3. "From the Sunny South," a kneeling Spanish girl with two tambourines and a hatted monkey. 4. "I'se Topsy," a little black girl seated with legs crossed, extra accessories are a straw hat and a Golliwog doll. **(Illustration 149.)** 5. "A Little Geisha," a kneeling Japanese girl with flowers; extra accessories are a fan and a doll. 6. "Minnehaha," a seated American Indian doll holding a bow and arrow; accessories include a quiver of arrows and a pot hanging from a tripod over a fire.

The seventh group consists of "Postcard No. 3396, Window Garden Series." It consists of a series of colorful and decorative flowers growing in flowerpots listed as follows: 1. Chrysanthemums. 2. Violets. 3. Crimson Rose Bush. 4. Forget-me-nots. 5. Purple and Gold Pansies and Assorted Flowers.

BELOW LEFT: Illustration 148. "Somebody's Sweetheart," one of six postcards from the "Mechanical Doll, Series I., Post card No. 3394." Basic markings on the back of the card are similar to those on the preceding postcard except for the number and the assembling directions. Size is 5½in x 3½in (14cm x 9cm). Jan Banneck Collection.

BELOW RIGHT: Illustration 149. "I'se Topsy," one of six postcards from "Mechanical Doll, Series II, Post card No. 3394." When cut out and assembled, the girl and her Golliwog sit upright in their flower garden. Markings on the back of the card are similar to those on preceding postcards, except for the assembling directions. Size is 5½in x 3½in (14cm x 9cm). Jan Banneck Collection.

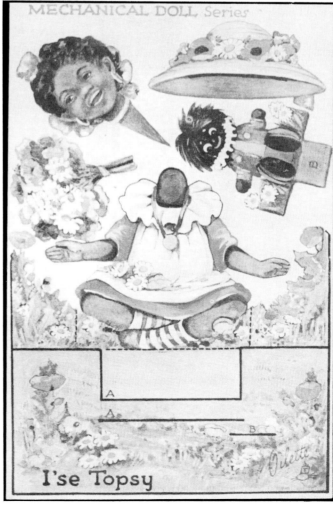

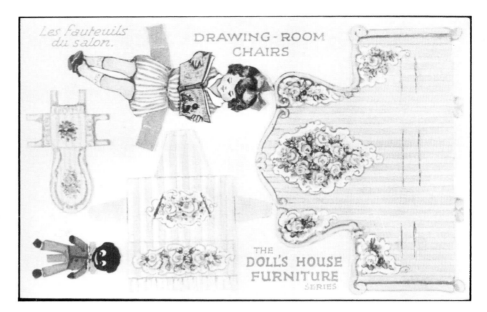

RIGHT: **Illustration 150.** *"Drawing-Room Chairs" from "The Doll's House Furniture Series, Post card No. 3398." When cut and assembled, the little girl sits in an armchair while Golliwog sits in a small chair. Markings on the back of the card are similar to those on the preceding card, except for card number and assembling instructions. Size 3½in x 5½in (9cm x 14cm). Jan Banneck Collection.*

The eighth group is "The Doll's House Furniture Series, Postcard No. 3398." The six cards are titled: 1. Baby in a Rocking Chair. 2. Drawing-Room Chairs. **(Illustration 150.)** 3. Drawing-Room Cabinet. 4. Drawing-Room Settee. 5. Grand-father Clock. 6. Ornamental Screen.

The ninth group is "Father Tuck's Toy Rockers, Postcard No. 3399." Each card has a rocker toy to be cut out and folded. The design has tabs to be inserted which may be cut out and included with the assembled rocking toy. 1. "Here we go up, up, up," a double-seated rocker holding a teddy bear and two dolls. The two smaller dolls may be placed in the laps of the two large dolls. **(Illustration 151.)** 2. "Little Tee Wee, Went to Sea in an Open Boat" pictures a girl in a boat with British flag and oars. A teddy bear and a doll are her passengers. Two additional small dolls may be cut out and become additional passengers. 3. "Peter Paddling His Canoe Round and Round the Lake," a boy sitting in a canoe holding a paddle. Two small dolls, one a clown, the other holding a pet cat, become passengers. 4. "Pussy-cat, Pussy-cat, Where Have You Been?" A cat on a hobby horse, a second cat on the platform beneath the horse. Two small kittens may be added to the toy. 5. "See a Fine Lady Upon a White Horse," a large doll sitting on a hobby horse with a Golliwog and another doll seated beneath the horse. Punch and Judy dolls may be cut out and added to the toy. 6. "This is the Way the Gentlemen Ride, Gallop-a-Trot, Gallop-

Illustration 151. *"Here we go up, up, up," one of six cards from "Father Tuck's Toy Rocker" Series No. 3399. A happy group sitting in a face-to-face rocker. Markings on the back of the card are similar to those on the preceding card, except for number and assembling directions. Size 5½in x 3½in (14cm x 9cm). Jan Banneck Collection.*

Illustration 152. *The "Clown" from the "Swinging Dolls" Series No. 3405. To be cut out, assembled and hung with string. Markings on the back of the card are similar to the six preceding cards, except for number and assembling directions. Size 3½in x 5½in (9cm x 14cm). Jan Banneck Collection.*

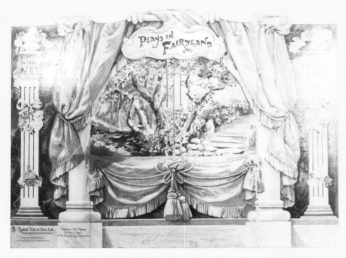

Illustration 153-A. A highly-colored and embossed theater proscenium with the title "Plays in Fairyland." Marked with the easel and palette trademark and "Raphael Tuck & Sons Ltd., London-Paris-Berlin-New York-Montreal, Publishers to Their Majesties The King & Queen and Her Majesty Queen Alexandra, Designed at the Studios in England and Printed at the Fine Art Works in Germany." The open extended size is 11⅞in high by 15⅝in wide (30cm x 40cm).

Illustration 153-B. Two of the principal characters from the old time favorite "Little Red Riding Hood," "Red Riding Hood" and the handsomely dressed "Wolf." Note how the over-sized die-cut characters fill the proscenium.

a-Trot," pictures a child riding a barrel-shaped horse with a clown doll and a girl doll riding below. A smaller clown doll and sailor doll may be added.

The tenth group, "Window Garden Series II, Postcard No. 3400" features six cards picturing the following potted plants: 1. Anemones. 2. Daffodils. 3. Hyacinths. 4. Poppies. 5. Sweet Peas. 6. Tulips.

The eleventh group is the "Flowers Fruit A.B.C. Series, Postcard No. 3402." It consists of six cards picturing letters of the alphabet, each with a flower or fruit. When cut out, each letter representing a fruit or flower will be made to stand. Card 1 pictures the letters A through D, card 2 the letters E through I, card 3 the letters J through M, card 4 the letters N through Q, card 5 the letters R through V and card 6 pictures letters W through Z.

The twelfth group is titled "Merry Little Men, Postcard No. 3403." We know of two of the six card set, "Nimble Niggers" and "Merry Music Makers."

The thirteenth group is titled "Model Railway Engines, Postcard No. 3404." We know of one of the six cards, the "London, Midland & Scottish Railway."

The fourteenth group is titled "Swinging Dolls, Postcard No. 3405." Each card has a half doll seated on a swing; the lower legs and accessories are separate. When cut out and assembled, following the directions on the back of the card, it becomes a swing toy. The six cards are titled: 1. "Clown." **(Illustration 152.)** 2. "Columbine." 3. "Harlequin." 4. "Joking Jock." 5. "Jolly Johny." 6. "Joyous Jenny." Don't question the spelling; its the way it appears on the cards.

There were other groups of postcards which we, unfortunately, have not seen. Possibly you may have some of them if you collect postcards of this type.

We would like to include a wonderful Tuck toy. It consists of a highly colored proscenium with the title "Plays in Fairyland." This three-section folded proscenium has its opening in the upper two-thirds of the center section. It is very similar to the box-like stages of the Punch & Judy show, although it is far more elaborate in exterior decoration. Heavy embossed red and pink curtains with yellow-gold fringe and cord and tassels frame the die-cut opening. On the outer extremities of the stage stand tall columns lightly decorated with red and yellow roses; all are highly embossed. Inside the opening are two hinged side scenes. The one on the left pictures a wooded area, the one on the right a broad path leading down to three steps. A wooded area is shown in the background. Colors are deep and brilliant and carry a high sheen. **(Illustration 153-A.)** Illustrations 153-B & C picture the colorful die-cut character figures of "Little Red Riding Hood" and a stylishly dressed "Wolf." The second group of characters represent the "Prince" offering "Cinderella" a crown.

Illustration 153-C. The two principal characters in the story of "Cinderella." Cinderella accepts the Prince's offer of marriage and they live happily ever after. There are no markings.

Chapter III

Part III

The Reign of King George V
and Queen Mary, 1910-1936
Paper Dolls Before and After World War I

The reign of King George V and Queen Mary began in 1910, after the death of George's father, King Edward. This reign encompassed the years 1910 through 1936. During this period of time World War I interrupted many business ventures. This is seen in the smaller production of published paper dolls by Raphael Tuck & Sons. There was also a vast difference in the material and colors used. Probably through necessity, after the war, the materials and colors were not of the same high quality usually published by Raphael Tuck & Sons.

After the reign of King Edward and Queen Alexandra, some of the markings on the paper dolls become somewhat confusing. This is because the title, "King and Queen," is often used with no reference to their exact names. The imprints on the paper dolls can be helpful in giving us the correct reign and date. We know that the Berlin office of Raphael Tuck & Sons was opened in 1907 and was closed in 1915. This leads us to believe that paper dolls marked with the name Berlin were definitely within the reign of George V and Queen Mary. Here again, the same rule of thumb applies to the paper dolls marked with the name of the city of Montreal. The Montreal office was in existence from 1907 through 1913. A few paper dolls during this reign have been found marked with the name of the city of Toronto. This marking is almost always printed with either the name Berlin or Montreal. According to the Metropolitan Toronto Reference Library, Raphael Tuck & Sons

Illustration 155. *"Bonnie Billy" No. 65 of the "Our Bonnie Series of Dressing Dolls." He is pictured with four of his outfits. He is marked with his series name, the Raphael Tuck easel and palette trademark, "Art Publishers to Their Majesties the King and Queen. Copyright by Raphael Tuck & Sons Co., Ltd., London, Paris, Berlin, Montreal, New York. Designed in the Studios in New York." Doll measures 9in (23cm). Maurine Popp Collection.*

Illustration 156. *"Bonnie Betty" No. 66 of the "Our Bonnie Series of Dressing Dolls." She is pictured with four of her outfits. She is marked with her series name and number, the Raphael Tuck easel and palette trademark, "Art Publishers to Their Majesties the King and Queen. Copyright by Raphael Tuck & Sons Co., Ltd., London, Paris, Berlin, Montreal, New York. Designed in the Studios in New York." Doll measures 9in (23cm). Maurine Popp Collection.*

first appeared in *Might's Toronto City Directory* in 1912 and the last entry was 1914 (no doubt because of World War I). The library also searched 1938-1950, but found nothing in Toronto directories, although Raphael Tuck & Sons Canada Limited was incorporated by the government of Canada on June 20, 1947. Another way to attempt to date the paper dolls from this period is through the costumes. *The Collector's Book of Dolls' Clothes* by the Colemans has a chapter titled "Wartime Dolls" that is very helpful.

Color Illustration XXXVII pictures "Fanny Fairleigh" of the "Maidens Fair Series of Dressing Dolls." Notice that the leg-o-mutton sleeves have disappeared and the skirts often appear to be pleated around the bottom. The slim waistlines are very apparent. The hats continue to be broad brimmed and lavishly decorated with feathers, flowers and ribbons. The costumes and hats are marked with the easel and palette trademark, "Patd. Feb. 20th 1894. Raphael Tuck & Sons Co., Ltd. New York, London, Paris, Berlin, Montreal. Art Publishers to Their Majesties the King and Queen. Designed at the Studios in New York and Printed in Germany."

Color Illustration XXXVIII pictures "Marion Manners" of the "Maidens Fair Series of Dressing Dolls." She is an adult paper doll, a thin-waisted brunette dressed in a long pink and white undergarment. Her four full-length costumes and broad-brimmed hats trimmed with feathers are moderate in color when compared with those of the younger generation. She is marked with the easel and palette trademark, "Patd. Feb. 20th 1894. Raphael Tuck & Sons Co., Ltd. New York, London, Paris, Berlin, Toronto. Designed at the Studios in New York and Printed in Germany." Her costumes are marked in the same way with the addition of the doll's series name.

Color Illustration XXIX is "Dorothy Dimples" from the "Maidens Fair Series of Dressing Dolls." This blonde child wears a short white chemise, white socks and low black strap shoes. She clutches a doll in her left hand. Her four outfits consist of a white Spring dress and bonnet trimmed with pink, a white Summer dress trimmed with green ribbon, a blue Fall dress with full sleeves and matching hat and a brown Winter outfit with matching fur muff, collar and cuffs and hat. She holds a snowball in her hand.

Color Illustration XXXVII. "Fanny Fairleigh," an adult paper doll from the "Maidens Fair Series of Dressing Dolls." The doll, costumes and hats are marked with the Tuck trademark and the patent date, Feb. 20th 1894. Other markings are: "Raphael Tuck & Sons Co., Ltd., New York, London, Paris, Berlin, Montreal. Art Publishers to Their Majesties the King and queen. Designed at the Studios in New York and Printed in Germany." Doll measures 12½in (32cm). Marlys Clark Collection.

Color Illustration XXXVIII. "Marion Manners," an adult paper doll from the "Maidens Fair Series of Dressing Dolls." The doll is marked with the Tuck trademark and patent date of Feb. 20, 1894. Additional markings are: "Raphael Tuck & Sons Co., Ltd., New York, London, Paris, Berlin, Toronto. Designed at the Studios in New York and Printed in Germany." All dresses are marked the same as the doll but with the addition of the doll's name and "Maidens Fair Series." Doll measures 12½in (32cm). Maurine Popp Collection.

Color Illustration XXXIX. *"Dorothy Dimples," a child paper doll from the "Maidens Fair Series of Dressing Dolls." Additional markings on the doll and her dresses and hats are: "Art Publishers to Their Majesties the King and Queen. Raphael Tuck & Sons Co., Ltd., New York, London, Paris, Berlin, Toronto. Designed at the Studios in New York and Printed in Germany." Doll measures 12½in (32cm).* Maurine Popp Collection.

ABOVE: *Illustration 157.* "Bonnie Babbie" No. 67 of the "Our Bonnie Series of Dressing Dolls." She is pictured with four of her outfits. She is marked with her series name and number, the Raphael Tuck easel and palette trademark, "Art Publishers to Their Majesties the King and Queen. Copyright by Raphael Tuck & Sons Co., Ltd., London, Paris, Berlin, Montreal, New York. Designed in the Studios in New York." Doll measures 9in (23cm). Maurine Popp Collection.

BELOW: *Illustration 158-B.* Jack Cranford with his four suits and hats, a two-piece suit, a sailor suit, a snowsuit and a winter coat. He is marked: "Jack, The Cranford Series of Dressing Dolls. Designed at the Studios in New York and Printed in Saxony." Doll measures 7½in (19cm). Maurine Popp Collection.

Illustration 158-A. The box cover for "Jack Cranford" of the "Cranford Children Series of Dressing Dolls." It mentions that he has four outfits. It is marked with the Tuck trademark, "Art Publishers to Their Majesties the King and Queen. Patd. Feb. 20th 1894. Raphael Tuck & Sons Co., Ltd., London, Paris, Berlin, Toronto, New York." Maurine Popp Collection.

159

The "Our Bonnie Series of Dressing Dolls" is a very appealing series that has one little boy and three little girls in it. They are all marked as follows: "Our Bonnie Series of Dressing Dolls." Raphael Tuck easel and palette trademark. "Art Publishers to Their Majesties the King and Queen. Copyright by Raphael Tuck & Sons Co., Ltd., London. Paris, Berlin, Montreal, New York. Designed at the Studios in New York." They all have their name and their number printed on the back. Their clothing is also marked with the trademark and "Copyright by Raphael Tuck & Sons Co., Ltd.," and numbered and lettered. Their numbers are 64 through 67.

Illustration 154 of the "Our Bonnie Series of Dressing Dolls" pictures "Bonnie Bessie" No. 64. She is pictured with four of her outfits. From left to right, they are: No. 64-A is a blue party dress trimmed with white lace and she carries a flower basket. No. 64-B is a peach-colored dress trimmed in royal blue. Her hat is straw. It is also trimmed in royal blue. She is carrying a doll. No. 64-C is a red coat with a fur collar and muff. No. 64-D is a red and white checked dress and she carries a teddy bear.

Illustration 155 pictures "Bonnie Billy," No. 65 of the "Our Bonnie Series of Dressing Dolls." He is pictured with four of his outfits. From left to right, they are: No. 65-A is a two-piece small checked suit with brown trim. He carries a schoolbook. No. 65-B is a light brown coat and hat. He holds snowballs in both hands. No. 65-C is a sailor suit and hat that is navy blue with a white collar. He holds a gun in his hands. No. 65-D is a two-piece suit. He has a white shirt, navy blue pants, a plaid tie and holds a toy horse and boat in his hands.

Illustration 156 is "Bonnie Betty" No. 66 of the "Our Bonnie Series of Dressing Dolls." She is pictured with four of her outfits. From left to right, they are: No. 66-A is a green coat and hat with a fur collar, muff and leggings. No. 66-B is a white party dress trimmed with pink bows. Her stockings are green. No. 66-C is a school dress with a sailor-type blouse. She appears to have schoolbooks in her arm. No. 66-D is a lavender-colored dress with a low waistline. She is carrying a bouquet of flowers.

Illustration 157 pictures "Bonnie Babbie," No. 67 of the "Our Bonnie Series of Dressing Dolls." She is also pictured with four of her outfits. From left to right, they are: No. 67-A is a pink party dress trimmed in white lace. She has long white gloves and carries flowers. No. 67-B is a red and white checked dress with a yolk of solid red fabric. Her stockings are black and she carries a package. No. 67-C is a blue pinafore with striped trim. Her hat is trimmed with daisies. No. 67-D is a royal blue coat with white fur, collar and muff.

Illustration 160. *"Jenny Cranford" with her four costumes. Left to right, top row, we see a white party dress trimmed with lace and blue ribbon and a blue dress with a white pinafore trimmed with blue braid. On the lower row, a green checked dress with a white underblouse and a white ermine coat and white and black high-button shoes. She is marked: "Jennie, The Cranford Series of Dressing Dolls. Designed at the Studios in New York and Printed in Saxony." Doll measures 7½in (19cm). Marlene Brenner Collection.*

ABOVE: Illustration 159. *"Jessie Cranford" with her four costumes. They are a white party dress, a blue romper suit, a green coat and a light brown coat. She is marked: "Jessie, The Cranford Series of Dressing Dolls. Designed at the Studios in New York and Printed in Saxony." Doll measures 7½in (19cm). Maurine Popp Collection.*

"The Cranford Children Series of Dressing Dolls" has four sets. They are "Jack Cranford," "Jennie Cranford," "Jessie Cranford" and "Jane the Nurse." It would be nice to know how these paper dolls came by the name "Cranford." Was this an imaginary name or the name of an actual family?

Illustration 158-A is the box cover for "Jack Cranford" of the "Cranford Children Series of Dressing Dolls." It carries his name and the series name plus these other markings: "1 doll, 4 dresses, 4 hats." The Tuck easel and palette trademark. "Art Publishers to Their Majesties the King and Queen. Patd. Feb. 20th 1894. Raphael Tuck & Sons Co., Ltd., London, Paris Berlin, Toronto, New York."

Illustration 158-B pictures "Jack Cranford" with his four suits and hats. Left to right is a two-piece suit, a sailor suit, a snowsuit (he is holding snowballs) and a winter coat with fur collar and cuffs and leggings. He is marked: "Jack, The Cranford Series of Dressing Dolls. Designed at the Studios in New York and Printed in Saxony."

Illustration 159 pictures "Jessie Cranford" with her costumes. Left to right is a white party dress trimmed with pink ribbon. She holds a fan in her hand. Next is a blue romper suit with white trim, then a green coat with brown trim and brown leggings with light brown trim and long leggings. Finally, she wears a brown fall outfit.

Illustration 160 pictures "Jennie Cranford" with her four costumes. Left to right, top row, we see a white party dress trimmed with lace and blue ribbon, a blue dress with a white pinafore trimmed with blue braid and on the lower row, a green checked dress with white underblouse and finally, a white ermine coat and white and black button shoes.

"Jane, The Nurse" is not pictured. Adding to the information about the Cranford Children, we would like to note here that all are marked in the same way except for their names.

Illustration 161 "Dollies On Their Travels" is a paper toy that must have given children a great deal of pleasure. When folded up, this toy measures 9-1/2in x 6in (24cm x 15cm). When opened, it measures 21in x 6in (53cm x 15cm). The folder is marked: "Contents, Four Dollies, One Trunk, One Suit Case, One Bag, Eight Dresses and Four Hats." Raphael Tuck trademark. "Art Publishers to Their Majesties the King and Queen. Raphael Tuck & Sons Co., Ltd., New York, London, Paris, Berlin, Toronto. Designed at the Studios in New York. Printed at the Fine Art Works in Saxony." The four dolls are attached to the scenery by their legs. Their backs and heads are loose so that the clothes and hats in the trunks can be put on and taken off. The piece in the foreground shows the construction of the backing of the clothes. The clothes are not marked.

Illustration 161. "Dollies On Their Travels" is a toy with four dolls, one trunk, one suitcase, one bag, eight dresses and four hats. Marked with the Raphael Tuck trademark, "Art Publishers to Their Majesties the King and Queen. Raphael Tuck & Sons Co., Ltd., New York, London, Paris, Berlin, Toronto. Designed at the Studios in New York. Printed at the Fine Art Works in Saxony." When folded up, it measures 9½in x 6in (24cm x 15cm). When opened, it measures 21in x 6in (53cm x 15cm).

Chapter IV

Part I

The Reign of George VI and Queen Elizabeth, 1936-1952

The Demise of a Great Publishing Firm

This was a period in which the company of Raphael Tuck & Sons suffered many ups and downs due to varying world events and changing economic conditions. Great Britain had passed through a period of depression when the very popular Prince of Wales, Edward, became king and then renounced the title.

In the late 1920s, the world's economy appeared to be reasonably sound and the employment rate was fairly stable. During this period, many people in the United States were dealing in the stock market, buying on margin. In 1929, the bottom fell out of the market and people faced a long period of depression. This dismal period lasted until the start of World War II, naturally having an effect on the overseas business of Raphael Tuck & Sons. During these years, Tuck's exports to the United States hit a low level. Americans were hard put to put food on their tables, let alone buy paper toys and other paper products.

The coming of World War II provided a dark cloud which hung over the firm of Raphael Tuck & Sons. The Germans had been delivering tides of air raids on Britain in 1940, and on the night of December 29th, unleashed one of their deadliest air raids of the war on London. The city became an inferno and when daylight came, a grim picture of destruction was viewed. What had been the headquarters of the Tuck firm the day before was now an empty shell of a building. During that fateful night, Desmond Tuck hurried from his home on the other side of London to see if anything could be salvaged. In a frantic effort, he managed to save an armful of items, the most important being the framed Royal Warrant of Appointment, granted to the Tuck firm through four reigns. The records of 74 years of the work of the firm were destroyed. The vast store of beautiful prints, postcards and various other paper products were gone. Everything of importance to conduct day-to-day business lay in a heap of burning ashes.

In the "corner stone," laid by Raphael Tuck 42 years before, was found a broken glass jar. Fortunately, the contents were intact. They included a catalog of Raphael Tuck & Sons early products and a booklet revealing the results of the Tuck Literary and Painting Competition of 1894. Also included was a copy of *The Times* and the *Daily Telegraph*, both dated April 5, 1898, some examples of greeting cards and periodicals and a history of the firm up until that time, written by Adolph Tuck.

It was a case of starting the firm from scratch. Some of the departments of the firm were established in temporary quarters in Appold Street E.C. and others in another building on Cromwell Road S.W. Supplies of materials were obtained and Raphael Tuck & Sons was again in business. As with many other businesses in the same situation, and despite wartime restrictions and shortages, they forged ahead.

As the war ended and many members of the former staff returned from war service, business and production momentum started to advance. In the period between 1945 and 1949, a number of important developments took place. The Tuck firm purchased a majority holding in Clarke & Sherwell Ltd., a well-known sheet-fed photogravure printer in Northampton. They opened up a second place of business in that same town and a new head office was established in the west end of London. In the following years, the development of new production and marketing techniques emerged and the firm seemed to be functioning strongly.

Sir Reginald Tuck passed away in 1954 and his son, Bruce, inherited the title, but was a member of the firm for a short period of time only. Desmond Tuck, Chairman and Managing Director during the mid 1950s, was the last of the Tuck family active in the firm's business. He carried on the affairs of business with a creative flair and energy much the way his father had earlier. He was active until he retired in 1959.

After the last Tuck left the firm, it seemed to change ownership a number of times. In 1962, Purnell & Sons Ltd., acquired the share capital in the firm and three years later, Raphael Tuck & Sons Ltd., and its subsidiary, Clarke & Sherwell Ltd., became member firms of the British Printing Corporation. During these various changes, the firm maintained a high standard of quality in all the items they published. However, the magic of the beautiful high quality color printing that they had formerly received from Germany up until the start of World War II was gone and so was the magic for collectors.

So ends the story that reads like a fantasy, the birth and growth of one of the world's great publishing houses, how it was affected by two wars and how it overcame these calamities and how it weakly emerged from World War II, but never regained its former high level of producing the earlier beautiful and unique paper items.

Chapter IV

Part II

The Reign of George VI
and Queen Elizabeth, 1936-1952
Paper Toys — Odds and Ends and Late Arrivals

Over the time period we took to write this book, we asked other collectors of paper dolls and toys if they had any Tuck material that could be used in our research. Fortunately, those asked did have some Tuck treasures and were happy to have them included in the book. Many of these loans were made early when we started and are in the proper time frames. Others arrived late and we are including them within this later period. Still others are only parts of sets which we find interesting and although only parts, are a part of the history of Raphael Tuck & Sons.

A complete boxed set in this category is from the Victorian period, titled "The Youngsters Library." The set contains 12 different panorama toy books. The box cover carries the title, No. 891 and is also marked: "Series I." This implies that there may have been others in the series. This set includes the following titles: "The Three Bears," "Punch & Judy," "Robinson Crusoe," "Clown Circus," "Water Circus," "Red Riding Hood," "Jack & the Beanstalk," "The Three Little Kittens," "Holiday Express" and "A Visit to the Zoo." The two remaining panoramas, "John Gilpin" and "A Visit to the Aquarium," were pictured earlier in Chapter I, Part II. These highly-colored six-section accordion-type panoramas were eye-catching, die-cut and embossed. **Illustration 162** pictures the box cover and the panorama titled "The Three Bears."

Illustration 162. "The Youngsters Library," a boxed set containing 12 folded, six-section panorama books. Each is highly colored, embossed and die-cut. The folded books measure 4½in x 3in (12cm x 8cm). The box is marked with the easel and palette trademark and "No. 891. Raphael Tuck & Sons, London-Paris-New York." Box size is 5in x 6¼in (13cm x 16cm). Maurine Popp Collection.

Another slightly later set is titled "Father Tuck's Picture Panoramas." It is marked: "Publishers to Their Majesties The King & Queen & TRH the Prince & Princess of Wales." The set consists of eight panoramas with the following titles: "The Toy Army," "Buttercup Farm," "Little Red Riding Hood," "Cinderella," "Forest & Jungle," "Three Little Kittens," "Beauty & the Beast" and "Feathered Friends." Each book panorama contains a page dealing with assembling instructions, four pages of story text, the colorful die-cut folded panorama and a card of perforated green cardboard stands. Pictured is the panorama titled "Feathered Friends" and the box cover. **(Illustration 163-A.)** Illustration 163-B pictures an informative slip found in the box. An example of one of these panoramas was mentioned and photographed previously, in its proper sequence. Having acquired this additional information, we felt it worthwhile to include it here.

A wonderful and unusual boxed set of lithographed paper on wood blocks is titled "Little Sweetheart Embossed Block." **(Illustration 164-A.)** The set consists of 12 flat blocks with the colorful illustrations applied to the two larger flat surfaces. Each side pictures two sets of six blocks. One side offers the titles "Ten Little Nigger Boys Going Out to Dine" and "Only to Say, How Do You Do & Introduce Myself to You" (a circus act). **(ILlustration 164-B.)** The opposite sides

Illustration 163-A. "Father Tuck's Panoramas." The set is made up of eight folded panoramas picturing a variety of subjects. The box cover is marked with the easel and palette mark and "Raphael Tuck & Sons, Ltd., London, Paris, New York, Montreal. Publishers to Their Majesties the King and Queen and T.R.H. The Prince and Princess of Wales." The box measures 5½in x 9½in x 1in (14cm x 24cm x 3cm). The folded 4¾in x 3in (12cm x 8cm) panorama opens out to 15in (38cm). Maurine Popp Collection.

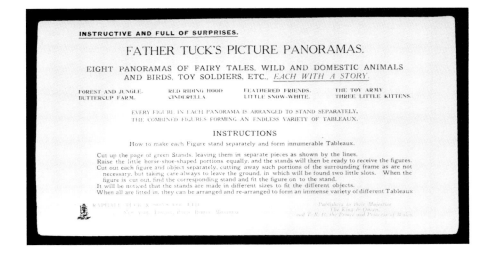

Illustration 163-B. The instruction sheet for Father Tuck's Picture Panoramas. Marked: "Instructive and Full of Surprises." Eight panoramas included in the set are: "Forest and Jungle," "Buttercup Farm," "Red Riding Hood," "Cinderella," "Feathered Friends," "Little Snow-White," "The Toy Army" and "Three Little Kittens." The sheet measures 5in high by 9in wide (13cm x 23cm). Maurine Popp Collection.

Illustration 164-A. The box cover of a set of 12 colorful lithographed paper on wood flat blocks. The cover label is unmarked except for the title. The box measures 14¾in high, 12¾in wide and ¾in deep (38cm x 32cm x 2cm). Richard Merrill Collection.

are titled " Water Circus" and "Jack & the Beanstalk." **(Illustration 164-C.)** Unusual features of the blocks are exactly the same as those used in a set of 12 different panorama toy books titled "The Youngsters Library." **(Illustration 162.)**

The next two items are wonderful stand-up novelties which feature a mirror. They are very similar to those pictured earlier in **Illustration 25.** The young man on the left wearing a long green coat and a top hat, frames the round mirror with his hands, the idea being that when the receiver of the card looks at it, she sees her reflection in the mirror. Above the mirror are the printed words: "To Me Luv" and below "A Leetle Burrd Told Me." This must have been a St. Patrick's Day card. The second two-section stand-up card features a young lady standing in front of her mirrored bureau. Above the mirror are the words "To Me Sweetheart" and across the rug at the base, the words "Oim waitin fer thee Love." **(Illustration 165.)**

A further example of a mechanical holiday card is the embossed and die-cut figure of a Chinese laundryman. This valentine figure has a double head and face movement, three pieces in all, fastened by a tiny cotter pin. The words: "Me likee you vellee much" are on his yellow costume. **(Illustration 166.)**

Included are a group of attractive holiday postcards picked from many thousands that Tuck published. The New Year card from Series 139 pictures two young ladies dressed in white winter outfits enjoying a walk through the falling snow. The St. Patrick's Day postcard pictures an Irish lassie holding a four-leaf clover over a young pig. The Easter postcard from Series 700 pictures a young lady in her Easter outfit holding a chick in her hands. The final card pictures a jolly Father Christmas holding a doll, looking in a window to see if a young girl would like her. This card was part of "Christmas Post Cards, Series 102." **(Illustration 167.)**

Two very nice die-cut valentines which are very different in art design are both equally appealing. One is a young lady in a striped violet and white dress with a plumed straw bonnet down and off her face. The second is a little Dutch Boy in a green and white outfit and a red and black hat. Both figures are equipped with a rear easel-type stand on which is printed a valentine message. **(Illustration 168.)**

Here is an outstanding example of Tuck salesmanship, encouraging American youngsters to become interested in postcards by painting their own. *The Children's*

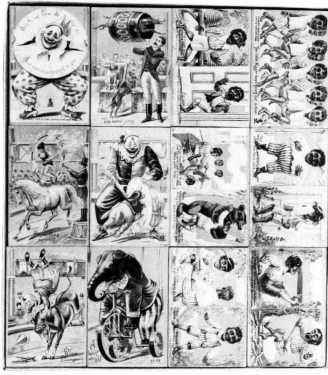

Illustration 164-B. One side of the two six block sets, that of the circus acts and the ten little black boys. The bottom of the first block in each set carries the words: "Raphael Tuck & Sons, London-Paris-New York. Designed in England, Printed in Germany." It also carries the easel and palette trademark. Each block measures 4¾in x 3in x ⅝in (12cm x 8cm x 1cm). Richard Merrill Collection.

Illustration 164-C. The under or reverse side, showing the third and fourth sides of the block sets titled "Water Circus" and "Jack and the Beanstalk." The wording along the bottom of the first block of each set and the block size are the same as those in the preceding illustration. Richard Merrill Collection.

BELOW: Illustration 165. *Two novelty St. Patrick's Day cards that feature a mirror. Both are two-piece cards jointed together with an accordion-type tab that, when spread, enables the cards to stand upright. Both cards are marked with the easel and palette trademark and "Raphael Tuck & Sons Ltd., Publishers to Their Majesties, London, Paris, Berlin, New York." The figures average 7in high and 4¼in wide (18cm x 11cm). Maurine Popp Collection.*

RIGHT: Illustration 167. *An assortment of colorful embossed holiday postcards for New Years, St. Patrick's Day, Easter and Christmas. All cards are marked with the easel and palette trademark and "Raphael Tuck & Sons. Art Publishers to Their Majesties The King and Queen." Cards measure 5⅜in high and 3½in wide (14cm x 9cm).*

LEFT: Illustration 166. *Possibly a novelty mechanical valentine, this comical Chinese laundryman has movable features on the face of a movable head which is attached to a long neck. The back is marked with the easel and palette trademark and "Publishers by Appointment to Their Majesties the King and Queen Alexandra, Raphael Tuck & Sons Ltd., London, Paris, New York. Designed at the Studios in England and Printed at the Fine Art Works in Germany." The figure stands 6¼in (17cm). Maurine Popp Collection.*

ABOVE: Illustration 168. *Two distinctly different die-cut valentines. Both are marked with the easel and palette trademark and "Raphael Tuck & Sons, Ltd., London, Paris, Berlin, New York, Toronto. Printed in Saxony." The attractive young lady in the large bonnet is 6¾in tall (17cm). The charming Dutch boy stands 8in tall (20cm).*

ABOVE: Illustration 169. *The cover of an unique coloring book titled* The Children's Postcard Painting Book *from Father Tuck's "Little Artists" series. The back cover is marked with the easel and palette trademark and "No. 6731. Published by Raphael Tuck & Sons, Co., Ltd., New York-London-Paris. Designed at the Studios in England." This book is 8¼in x 6⅛in (21cm x 16cm).*

ABOVE RIGHT: Illustration 170. *The cover of the booklet titled* Some Cats For Painting, *cats drawn by Louis Wain. The booklet is marked with the easel and palette trademark and "Raphael Tuck & Sons Ltd., London-Paris-Berlin-New York-Toronto. Publishers to Their Majesties The King and Queen and Her Majesty Queen Alexandra. No. 4082. Designed at the Studios in England and Printed at the Fine Art Works in Bavaria." Booklet measures 7in high by 6in wide (18cm x 15cm).*

Post Card Painting Book is an 11-page soft cover book. The inside front and back covers list "Instructions for Little Artists." The interior pages show the full color illustrations on the left with line drawings on the right which are to be painted in. The reverse side is the address side of the postcard, two to a page. The cards are separated by perforated lines so that they might be carefully torn out. Hence, a child could paint in their own postcard, address it, apply a stamp and send it through the mail to a friend. This particular paint book is marked for the American market. See the book cover pictured in **Illustration 169.**

A second postcard painting book similar to the one above is titled "Some Cats For Painting" by Louis Wain. This soft cover book contains eight pages, two cards to a page. Odd number pages picture color portraits of cats; even number pages contain line drawings of the same cats to be painted in. The reverse side of all cards are in the form of the standard address side of a Tuck postcard. **(Illustration 170.)**

An interesting group of characters, both young and old, are pictured in **Illustration 171.** The three pieces of scrap are titled "The Christening." They show the heads of the family members along with those of "The Rector," "Nurse," and the "Pew Opener." Family members pictured top row, left to right, are: "Papa," "Mama" and "God Father." Middle row: "God Mother," "The Infant" and bottom row, "Aunt Fanny," "Cousin Tom," "Brother Billy" and "Bumble."

A late find was an early most enjoyable book published during Queen Victoria's reign. Titled *The Dog that would a Soldier be*, it tells a story in verse of a dog named Terrier Fox and his love for Lady Constantine Caroline King. The story took place during a period when all dogs were enlisting in the Royal Army in order to declare war on the enemy, the Cat Army. Terrier Fox joins the army and the terrible battle starts, finally coming to an end with both sides suffering many casualties. The Dog Army marches home in victory. Terrier Fox is one of the casualties, having lost an eye and one leg. He returns to Lady Constantine and she greets her lover with the following quote: "Half a lover by my side is better than a dead one." This is an outstanding satire on war portrayed by dogs. The verses and the seven full-page illustrations bring out the emotional feelings of happiness, sorrow and love, qualities found in life. This is a wonderful piece of work by the author, H. G. F. Taylor and artist, Allanson Cull. **(Illustrations 172-A & 172-B.)**

We now move from one of the great pieces of the Victorian Period to one of Raphael Tuck & Sons last toy publishing achievements. It is a magnificent 4ft

THE CHRISTENING. Painted by George Cruikshank

PEW OPENER   PAPA   MAMA   GOD FATHER

GOD MOTHER   THE INFANT   NURSE.   THE RECTOR

AUNT FANNY.   COUSIN TOM   BROTHER BILLY   BUMBLE.

Illustration 171. Three strips of "scrap." It is titled "The Christening" and shows the portraits or heads of a family gathering at a christening. Top row, left to right: "Pew Opener," "Papa," "Mama" and "God Father." Middle row: "God Mother," "The Infant," "Nurse" and "The Rector." Bottom row: "Aunt Fanny," "Cousin Tom," "Brother Billy" and "Bumble." They are marked "RT&S" and "Painted by George Cruikshank." Each strip measures 2in x ¼in (5cm x 11cm). Lorna Lieberman Collection.

(1.2m) long panorama depicting the 1952 Coronation Procession of Queen Elizabeth II. This wonderful four-section folding panorama is equipped with a series of horizontal slots which accept a large number of figures and objects. These include some 27 mounted cavalrymen and a strip containing eight Windsor Greys horses pulling the State Coach. On the near horses, those on the left, ride Postillions in red and gold uniforms. Beside the horses march the Grooms in Coronation liveries of red and gold. Beside the coach itself stride representatives of the Yeomen of the Guards. The background of the Royal Procession is supplemented by 18 towering poles equipped with colorful banners and three long platoons of scarlet-coated guardsmen. All these figures are inserted into various horizontal slots. In the background, on the far right, stands the Queen Victoria Memorial, surrounded by another platoon of scarlet-coated guards with tall bearskin headgear. Beyond this group and a bit to the right stands Buckingham Palace.

On the back of two of the four panels is a printed account of the Royal Procession, the Coronation itself and those personalities who took part in the festive events that took place June 2, 1952. The back section of the folded panorama is so constructed that it forms an envelope which holds the colorful die-cut models of the Coronation Coach, horses and riders, guardsmen, banners, buildings and so forth. **Illustration 173** pictures the cover of this colorful "Coronation Procession Panorama."

Illustration 172-A. *The cover of a wonderful book titled* The Dog that would a Soldier be, *illustrated by Allanson Cull. It is marked with the easel and palette trademark, "No. 1091" and "Raphael Tuck & Sons, London, Paris and New York. Publishers to Her Majesty the Queen, Designed at the Studios in England. Printed in Bavaria." Size is 9½in x 12¾in (24cm x 32cm).*

Illustration 172-B. *"An Army Bold to go and smash up Catland" is the title of this parade scene. One of seven full-page amusing full color illustrations from the book* The Dog that would a Soldier be." *Size is 9½in x 12¾in (24cm x 32cm).*

Illustration 173. *One of Raphael Tuck & Sons last paper toys titled "Coronation Procession Panorama." Marked with the easel and palette trademark and "Printed and Published by Raphael Tuck & Sons Ltd., Fine Art Publishers by Appointment to the Late King George VI, H.M. Queen Elizabeth The Queen Mother and H.M. Queen Mary. Copyright, Printed and made in England." Size is 10in x 12in (25cm x 31cm). Maurine Popp Collection.*

Chapter IV

Part III

The Reign of George VI and Queen Elizabeth, 1936-1952
Tuck's Latest Paper Dolls

Unfortunately, we have very few examples of paper dolls for this period and we have very little knowledge of how many sets Tuck published during this time. The examples we have may be characterized as colorful and cute, but they lack the depth of color and the imagination found in the earlier paper dolls by the Tuck firm.

"Little Playmates, Bonnie Bertie and Merry Madge" is the title of a boxed set containing two darling paper dolls with eight changes of costume and accessories. **(Illustration 174-A.)** Each die-cut doll stands 8¼in (21cm) tall. Each costume, bonnet and accessory is simply marked and numbered, geared for littler girls eight years old or younger. The artwork is the work of Anes Richardson. The box cover pictures the two appealing dolls dressed for a walk. **(Illustration 174-B.)**

Three rather similar boxed sets titled "Father Tuck's Dressing Doll Series," number 4, 3 and 2 are pictured in **Illustration 175.** Each of these boxed sets contains an 8¾ (22cm) die-cut doll identical to the one pictured on the above box covers, plus six different costumes and matching hats for each doll. Each costume represents a favorite fairy tale or nursery rhyme character. For example, the costumes in Series I represent those of the Queen of Hearts, Snow White, Miss Muffet, Cinderella and Red Riding Hood. The artist is listed at the bottom of each box as follows: "Fairy Tale and Nursery Rhyme Favourites by Dinah."

This same series of paper dolls was published in booklet form under the title *Raphael Tuck & Sons Dressing Doll Story Book for Young People.* **(Illustration 176-**

Illustration 174-A. The colorful contents of a set titled "Little Playmates, Bonnie Bertie and Merry Madge." The contents are unmarked except for a letter and a number on each part showing which costume or accessories go with Bertie and Madge. This set was geared for the six to eight-year-old child. Each die-cut doll is 8¼in tall (21cm). Jan Banneck Collection.

Illustration 174-B. The box cover of the "Little Playmates" set showing the dolls "Bertie and Madge" dressed in their winter outfits. The cover carries the easel and palette mark and "No. 395" plus "Raphael Tuck & Sons Ltd., Publishers to Their Majesties the King and Queen. Designed at the Studios in England. Printed at the Fine Art Works in Bavaria." Box size 9¼in high, 12in wide and 3/4in deep (24cm x 30cm x 2cm). Jan Banneck Collection.

Illustration 175. The covers of three boxed sets, each containing an 8¾in die-cut paper doll, each doll with six costumes and hats. Each box and doll and costume is marked with the Tuck trademark. Each piece carries the additional markings: "Raphael Tuck & Sons Ltd., Fine Art Publishers to Their Majesties the King and Queen and to her Majesty Queen Mary, London and Northampton, New York, Toronto." Box measures 11¼in x 5¼in x 1in (29cm x 13cm x 3cm).

BELOW: Illustration 176-A. The cover of the booklet titled "Dressing Doll Story Book for Young People." It carries the Tuck trademark and "Raphael Tuck & Sons Ltd., Fine Art Publishers to T.M. the King and Queen and to H.M. Queen Mary. Printed in England." Booklet size is 11¾in x 9⅝in (30cm x 25cm).

BELOW RIGHT: Illustration 176-B. An inside color page of the uncut paper dolls from the booklet titled "Raphael Tuck & Sons Dressing Doll Story Book for Young People." Directions for cutting out and gluing stands on the back of the dolls are given to make them stand upright. The backs of the dolls carry the name of the doll only. Page size is 11¾in x 9⅝in (30cm x 25cm).

A.) It contains eight colorful paper dolls and 24 costumes along with the appropriate head wear. It is marked: "Designing and Art Work by DINAH." These dolls and costumes, to be cut out, were smaller in size than the previously mentioned sets. The uncut dolls are 4½in (12cm) high. **(Illustration 176-B.)** Each dressed doll is accompanied by a short story or some lines in verse. The costumes represent those worn by favorite fairy tale characters such as Robin Hood, Lucy Locket, Sinbad, Jack the Giant Killer and the like. The booklet contains 16 pages, half of uncut paper dolls and their costumes and half of the story text.

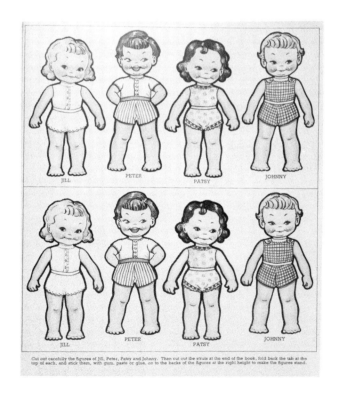

Bibliography

Fawcett, Clara Hallard. *Paper Dolls A Guide to Costume.* N.Y.: H. L. Lindquist Publications, 1951.

Ferguson, Barbara Chaney. *The Paper Doll.* Des Moines, Ia.: Wallace Homestead Book Company, 1982.

Howard, Marian. *Those Fascinating Paper Dolls.* Rev. Ed. N.Y.: Dover Publications, Inc., 1980.

Jendrick, Barbara Whitton. *Paper Dolls and Paper Toys of Raphael Tuck & Sons.* Bridgewater, Ct.: Privately printed, 1970.

_____. *A Picture Book of Paper Dolls and Paper Toys.* Bridgewater, Ct.: Privately printed, 1974.

Musser, Cynthia Erfurt. *Precious Paper Dolls.* Cumberland, Md.: Hobby House Press, Inc., 1985.

Spinning Wheel's Complete Book of Dolls. Hanover, Pa.: Everybody's Press, Inc., 1975.

Wallach, Anne Tolstoi. *Paper Dolls.* N.Y.: Van Nostrand Reinhold Company, Inc., 1982.

Whitton, Blair. *Paper Toys of the World.* Cumberland, Md.: Hobby House Press, Inc., 1986.

Midwest Paper Dolls & Toys Quarterly. Box 131, Galesburg, Ks 66740.

INDEX

Figures given in italic type are illustration numbers, not page numbers.